MALACHI:

Messenger of Rebuke and Renewal

D0170384

MALACHI:

Messenger of Rebuke and Renewal

David M. Levy

The Friends of Israel Gospel Ministry, Inc.
P. O. Box 908, Bellmawr, New Jersey 08099

MALACHI: Messenger of Rebuke and Renewal

David M. Levy

Copyright © 1992 by The Friends of Israel Gospel Ministry, Inc.
Bellmawr, NJ 08099

Fourth Printing..2008

Library of Congress Catalog Card Number: 91-77554
ISBN-10 0-915540-20-7
ISBN-13 978-0-915540-20-4

Cover by Design Point, Inc., Salem, OR.

Visit our Web site at *www.foi.org*

DEDICATION

To my parents
Beulah Ruth and Irving M. Levy

Loving and patient parents who stood with me during the formative years of my development and kept me focused toward a life of meaning and purpose.

CONTENTS

MALACHI OUTLINE

PREFACE

Often the books of the prophets are viewed as antiquated historical literature, penned millennia ago by seers whose messages have little application to men living in the 20th century. Nothing could be further from the truth. The minor prophets are a treasure trove of practical truths whose timeless messages speak to the human condition, whether it be social, political, or religious.

Malachi is this sort of book. Although short in content and last in the list of prophetic writings, it is long on meaty teaching of godly principles and by no means least in importance. The prophet's message is as contemporary and convicting to men in our age as it was 2,500 years ago.

The book opens with a declaration of God's unconditional love for an elect Israel—a love that the nation continually questioned, doubted, and mocked in a spirit of insensitivity and indifference. Not only did Israel profane the name and worship of God, but the men broke their marriage covenants and became unequally yoked with heathen women, robbed God of His rightful tithes and offerings, and committed hypocrisy by pretending to live dedicated lives before the Lord while, in reality, practicing wickedness.

Most likely this indifference was precipitated by the example of a corrupt clergy who compromised their call and polluted both the sacrifice and the sanctuary in which they served. Malachi warned the priests that unless true repentance was forthcoming, judgment would fall on all of Israel.

To the righteous within the nation, the prophet offered a word of hope. God would send His messenger to prepare the

1

way for the Messiah, who would come to purify both the Temple and the priesthood.

Malachi ended his prophecy with a final warning concerning "the day of the LORD," which will include the coming of Elijah and the Messiah, who will judge the wicked and deliver the righteous.

An understanding of the Book of Malachi is of paramount importance for at least three reasons. First, it profiles the religious, social, and political issues Judah faced after their return from the Babylonian captivity. Second, Malachi was the last of the Old Testament prophets to herald God's message of judgment against sin and the glorious kingdom that awaits the righteous at the Messiah's coming. Third, it was the final authentic voice of prophecy until John the Baptist shattered the silence 400 years later with the words, "Repent; for the kingdom of heaven is at hand" (Mt. 3:2).

INTRODUCTION

Background

Malachi was the last Old Testament book to be penned. It was written about one hundred years after Cyrus decreed that Judah could return to their land (538 B.C.). During that time the Jewish faith was reformed under Ezra and Nehemiah, but soon the priests and people became apathetic, indifferent, and morally corrupt. Malachi revealed Judah's sins and proclaimed that judgment would be forthcoming unless the people returned to God.

Author

Malachi means *my messenger* or *my angel* and is not mentioned outside of this book. Thus, some scholars believe that Malachi cannot be used as a proper name but refers only to the office of messenger. They believe that verse 1 should read: "The burden of the word of the LORD to Israel by *my messenger*." Other arguments are presented as a basis for their position. First, Jewish Targums consider the term *Malachi* to refer to the office of messenger. Second, Haggai, Zechariah, and Malachi were contemporaries of Ezra and Nehemiah, but only Haggai and Zechariah are mentioned in the two historical books. Space restrictions here do not permit refutation of the above arguments and others presented by critics, but none of them has proven to be valid. The content of the book indicates that it was written by a prophet, and there is no reason to doubt that it was Malachi. Nothing is known of Malachi's personal background.

Content

The text is divided into four chapters in the English translation but only three chapters in the Hebrew Bible. Chapter 1 begins with a declaration of God's love for Israel, but the nation is indifferent, questioning His love for them. This indifference is manifested by the priests, who pollute the sacrifice, the sanctuary, and their service to God. Chapter 2 indicates that the priests will be judged if they refuse to repent. Chapter 3 declares that God will send His messenger to prepare the way for the Messiah, who will come to purify both the Temple and the priesthood as well as to judge the wicked. The people are accused of robbing God but are told that if they pay their tithes and reform their practices, He will bless them. Chapter 4 is a final warning before the Day of the Lord, which will include the coming of Elijah and the Messiah, who will judge the wicked and deliver the righteous.

Date

Malachi did not date the writing of his prophecy, but evidence indicates that it was written after the fall of Babylon to Cyrus (538 B.C.). Judah seemed to be living under a Persian governor (1:8). The Temple worship had been restored (1:7-8, 10), and there is no mention of idolatry being practiced, as before their captivity. A moral and spiritual decline of the people paralleled the time of Ezra (458 B.C.) and Nehemiah (445 B.C.), including intermarriage with Gentiles (2:10-12; Ezra 9:1-2) and oppression of the poor (3:5; Neh. 5:4-5). The Nabataeans had defeated the Edomites (1:1-4), who were in turn defeated early in the fifth century B.C. Therefore, Malachi had to be written sometime between 433 and 400 B.C.

Style

Malachi's style is different from that of other prophetic writers. He did not write in poetic language but in pointed, easy-to-understand, exalted prose. The form is what some call a running disputational dialogue. There are usually three parts to this style: God questioned Israel about her spiritual condition, often beginning with the words, "ye say"; Israel countered, claiming innocence, with an inadequate, flippant answer; God refuted their reply.

MALACHI 1:1-5

The burden of the word of the LORD to Israel by Malachi. I have loved you, saith the LORD. Yet ye say, In what way hast thou loved us? Was not Esau Jacob's brother? saith the LORD; yet I loved Jacob, And I hated Esau, and laid his mountains and his heritage waste for the jackals of the wilderness. Whereas Edom saith, We are impoverished, but we will return and build the desolate places, thus saith the LORD of hosts, They shall build, but I will throw down; and they shall call them, The border of wickedness, and, The people against whom the LORD hath indignation forever. And your eyes shall see, and ye shall say, The LORD will be magnified from the border of Israel.

chapter 1

A PEOPLE DIVINELY LOVED

In 1916, F. M. Lehman penned a hymn he titled "The Love of God." Touched by words scribbled on the wall of a mental institution, he incorporated them into the last stanza of his hymn. The lyrics read like this:

Could we with ink the ocean fill,
And were the skies of parchment made,
Were ev'ry stalk on earth a quill,
And ev'ry man a scribe by trade,
To write the love of God above,
Would drain the ocean dry.
Nor could the scroll contain the whole,
Tho' stretched from sky to sky.

One could replace the word *above* and make the phrase read "to write the love of God to Israel" and be theologically correct, for God's love to Israel permeates the whole revelation of His Word to man.

Malachi was about to unfold God's love for Israel. But before doing so, he introduced his prophecy with the phrase, "The burden of the word of the LORD to Israel by Malachi" (v. 1). The word *burden* (*massa*) has the idea of something heavy, a load to be lifted up. It is the equivalent of *a weighty word full of meaning*. The message Malachi was about to deliver had divine authority behind it, for it was "the word of the LORD." "LORD" (*Yahweh*) is the name used to express God's covenant relationship with Israel, to which covenant she was unfaithful.

Malachi addressed his message "to Israel." But how could this be, for the Assyrians had destroyed Israel (the ten northern tribes) in 722 B.C.? The words *to Israel* referred to both the ten northern tribes and the two southern tribes, Judah and Benjamin.

It must be remembered that not all Israel (only the leadership and military establishment) were deported to Assyria in 722 B.C. Years later Hezekiah called the remnant of Israel (left in the land) to come and keep the Passover in Jerusalem (2 Chr. 30:18). Many came from the tribes of Ephraim, Manasseh, Issachar, and Zebulun (2 Chr. 11:16-17) and identified themselves with the house of David (2 Chr. 19:4; 30:1, 10-11, 25-26; 35:17-18). We can therefore draw several conclusions. First, all the tribes were represented after the Assyrian invasion. Second, all the tribes were represented in Judah when they returned to the land after the Babylonian captivity (536 B.C.), for they are called "Israel" (2 Chr. 12:6; 21:2; 28:19). Third, Christ offered Himself to "the lost sheep of the house of Israel" (Mt. 10:6)—that is, to all the tribes. Fourth, the tribes existed in the land during the New Testament times (Mt. 4:13, 15; Lk. 2:36; Acts 4:36; Phil. 3:5; Jas. 1:1). Fifth, in Acts 2, Peter used the terms "Jews" (v. 5), "Judea" (v. 14), "men of Israel" (v. 22), and "house of Israel" (v. 36) as synonyms. Thus, the 12 tribes are represented within the tribe of Judah and were not destroyed or lost, as some teach today.

Love Declared

Malachi wasted no time declaring God's true feelings for His people: "I have loved you, saith the LORD" (v. 2). The word *love* is in the Hebrew perfect tense, indicating that God not only loved Israel in the past but loves them in the present as well.

There are several aspects to God's love for Israel. First, His love is unconditional, for it was an act of pure grace, not dependent on anything Israel had done (Dt. 7:7-8; 10:15; 23:5). Second, God's love was sovereignly bestowed. He called Abraham from Ur of the Chaldeans, made a covenant with him, and confirmed it through Isaac and Jacob. Third, God's love for Israel is everlasting (Jer. 31:3)—a commitment He has not made with any other nation. His compassion for Israel

12

is like that of a mother for her child. In fact, God has engraved them on the palms of His hands (Isa. 49:14-16). Fourth, God's love for Israel is like that of a husband and wife (2:11). Fifth, God's love for Israel is like a father's love for his son (1:6; 3:17). On two occasions He called Israel His son (Ex. 4:22; Hos. 11:1).

Scripture pictures Israel as the apple of God's eye (Dt. 32:10), which literally means the pupil of the eye. When we look into the eye of another, that person's pupil acts as a mirror reflecting our image. In this passage, the Jew is the reflected image from the pupil of God's eye. Israel is so precious in God's sight that the Lord protects them from danger as He would His own eye. When the Jew is afflicted, God feels it as if it had happened to Him.

Love Debated

How did Israel respond to the declaration of God's love? Malachi verbalized what the nation felt: "Yet ye say, In what way hast thou loved us?" (v. 2). There are several possible reasons why Israel questioned God's love. The prophets had proclaimed that the kingdom would be restored to Israel upon their return to the land, but they were still under the control of a foreign power. Neither did they enjoy the expected prosperity that the prophets had predicted would accompany a return to the land. True, the Temple had been rebuilt, but its splendor was nothing like that of Solomon's Temple. Therefore, an embittered people questioned God's love for them.

How could the people respond with these stunning words to an expression of God's love for them, especially after they had experienced such privilege, protection, and personal blessing from God? He had restored the land, allowed them to reestablish the Temple and its worship, brought revival under Ezra and Nehemiah, and given them rest from their enemies. Often an ungrateful heart blinds a person or a people to what God has bestowed on them.

Where love is most manifested, it is often least appreciated. Often we see this in the family context—between husband and wife or children and parents. We see it also in nations—people who have received great blessing from God question His concern for them during difficult times. We see it in the lives of Christians greatly loved and blessed who question His love for them during times of extended trial or loss.

Although God was under no obligation to entertain such an insensitive question, because He is long-suffering He responded in love, not judgment.

Love Demonstrated

Esau and Jacob

God refuted Israel's charge about His lack of love by referring to Jacob's election over Esau: "Was not Esau Jacob's brother? saith the LORD; yet I loved Jacob" (v. 2). Esau and Jacob were twin brothers, but Esau, being the firstborn, had the privilege of primogeniture. Yet God intervened and chose Jacob to receive the birthright and blessing instead.

Not only did God love Jacob, but He contrasted that love with the statement, "And I hated Esau" (v. 3). How should we interpret this seemingly harsh statement? Some believe the word *hate* should be taken at face value. God meant what He said. He hated Esau because of his wicked deeds and those of his descendants. Others believe that the words *love* and *hate* should be used in a relative sense. God loved Jacob so much that, in comparison, it seemed as if He hated Esau, or *loved him less.* Still others believe that one cannot determine what God really meant by the statement because no interpretation is given. Scripture seems to substantiate the second position, as illustrated by Jacob's marriages to Rachel and Leah. Jacob loved Rachel, but he "hated" Leah (Gen. 29:30-33). Does this mean that Jacob actually hated Leah, his wife? No! It simply means that he loved Rachel much more than Leah. A better translation of the word *hated* in this context is *unloved.* We see the same illustration presented under the Law about a man who had two wives (Dt. 21:15-17).

Jesus presented this same idea in relation to salvation. The individual must "hate" his family and self or he cannot be Jesus' disciple (Lk. 14:26). Naturally, He did not mean that we should hate family members but, rather, *love them less*, as clarified in Matthew 10:37: "He that loveth father or mother more than me, is not worthy of me; and he that loveth son or daughter more than me, is not worthy of me."

Paul used the love/hate contrast to illustrate God's sovereign election of Jacob over Esau in Romans 9:10-15:

> When Rebecca also had conceived by one, even by our father, Isaac (For the children being not yet born, neither having done any good or evil, that the purpose of God according to election might stand, not of works, but of him that calleth), It was said unto her, The elder shall serve the younger. As it is written, Jacob have I loved, but Esau have I hated. What shall we say then? Is there unrighteousness with God? God forbid. For he saith to Moses, I will have mercy on whom I will have mercy, and I will have compassion on whom I will have compassion.

God was not speaking on an emotional level, as if He were more fond of one than the other. Rather, He spoke about His sovereign choice of Jacob and his descendants to carry out His spiritual purposes. Someone has said, "The difficult question is not why God would say that He hated Esau, but how could He say He loved Jacob?"

Often Jacob is pictured as a shrewd schemer who stole his brother's birthright and blessing. Esau, on the other hand, is looked upon as a rugged outdoorsman, simple in his understanding, who was taken in by a crafty brother.

We must remember that God revealed to the parents that He had reversed the order—"the elder shall serve the younger" (Gen. 25:23). Before the Law, there was no commandment

15

stating that the birthright and blessing were to go to the firstborn, although it was customary to do so.

God knew the characters of Esau and Jacob before their birth. He knew that Esau would have no interest in spiritual things, that he would marry two heathen women (a Hittite and a Hivite), and that he would later be called a fornicator and profane person (Heb. 12:16). Jacob, on the other hand, is described as a "quiet man" (Gen. 25:27), which meant that he was sincere or complete. Actually, Jacob was a righteous man who had a concern for the family birthright and blessing. He was much better prepared to carry out the spiritual leadership of the family, since Esau despised his birthright (Gen. 25:34). Thus, God had ordained that Jacob receive both the birthright and the blessing.

Because Isaac would not have bestowed the blessing on Jacob (which was God's design), Rebekah devised a plan to bring it about. Jacob did not want to go through with his mother's planned deception, but he remained obedient to her parental authority when she agreed to be responsible for the outcome of her actions (Gen. 27:13). After he received the blessing, God revealed Himself to Jacob in a dream. During the dream, God never rebuked him for the manner in which he obtained the blessing from his father. In fact, He pronounced more blessing on Jacob (Gen. 28:12-15).

God's Love for Israel

What God does or allows to happen is right, although His actions may seem incongruous to finite man. God not only hated Esau, but He "laid his mountains and his heritage waste for the jackals of the wilderness" (v. 3). The term *mountains* refers to the land of the Edomites, who were Esau's descendants. They were decimated by the Babylonians in 586 B.C. and the Nabataean Arabs sometime between 550 and 400 B.C. The Nabataeans intermingled with a remnant of the Edomites and became a mighty power (southeast of Judea) until the Romans destroyed them around 100 A.D. The Romans referred to the Edomites as Idumaeans, of whom King Herod was a descendant.

Why did God destroy Edom? The Edomites were an immoral and godless people who continually oppressed Israel (Gen. 36:1-8; Heb. 12:16). At least seven events led to their destruction. First, they refused to allow Moses passage through their land during Israel's pilgrimage to Canaan. Second, many of Israel's kings, including Saul, David, Solomon, Jehoshaphat, and Jehoram, fought the Edomites because of their opposition to Israel. Third, Edom did not help or even offer to assist Judah when they were invaded by foreign powers who carried off the treasure of Jerusalem. Fourth, she rejoiced over Judah's captivity. Fifth, Edom looted Jerusalem after her destruction. Sixth, she helped set up roadblocks to prevent Jewish people from fleeing their enemies. Seventh, she delivered the people of Judah to their captors. God severely judged the Edomites for their violence toward Israel.

The Edomites were an arrogant people who considered their land to be impregnable. How wrong they were! Even after their conquest, they still exuded pride and confidence in their ability to rebuild Edom: "We will return and build the desolate places" (v. 4).

But the Lord had the final word: "They shall build, but I will throw down; and they shall call them, The border of wickedness, and, The people against whom the LORD hath indignation forever" (v. 4). Although other nations might fall and rise again, Edom would not survive as a people because of their violence toward Judah (Joel 3:19).

Israel questioned God's love and was bitter because He had allowed the Babylonians to take them captive and permitted the Edomites to add to their sorrow (Ps. 137:7). God proved His love for Israel by choosing Jacob over Esau and destroying the Edomites, who would never rise again.

Love Diffused

Although Israel was insensitive and indifferent to God's love and grace, there will come a day when they will be forced to acknowledge it: "And your eyes shall see, and ye shall say, The LORD will be magnified from the border of Israel" (v. 5).

The word *from* can be translated *above* or *beyond* the border of Israel. Both interpretations are possible, but the context indicates that *beyond* is preferable, because God's name will be great among the nations (vv. 11, 14). Thus, God's love transcends national boundaries and is extended beyond Israel to all nations. We see God's love for all nations in the covenant He made with Abraham: "In thee shall all families of the earth be blessed" (Gen. 12:3). This promise was fulfilled in Jesus Christ, who is the means of spiritual redemption to mankind:

> And the scripture, forseeing that God would justify the Gentiles through faith, preached before the gospel unto Abraham, saying, In thee shall all nations be blessed . . . Now to Abraham and his seed were the promises made. He saith not, And to seeds, as of many; but as of one. And thy seed, which is Christ (Gal. 3:8, 16).

God has chosen a great multitude from the nations and forged them into "a chosen generation, a royal priesthood, an holy nation, a people of his own" (1 Pet. 2:9), which He calls the Church. God's divine purpose for both Israel and the Church is that they shall show forth His praise throughout the world.

P. P. Bliss, the evangelistic singer and composer, was in a meeting where the song "O How I Love Jesus" was continually being sung. Upon reflection, he was struck with the idea of how much God loved him in comparison to his love for God. Quickly he wrote the lyrics of "Jesus Loves Even Me." His second stanza captured the theme of Malachi's messege to Israel and all men:

> Though I forget Him and wander away,
> Still He doth love me wherever I stray;
> Back to His dear loving arms would I flee,
> When I remember that Jesus loves me.

I am so glad that Jesus loves me! Are you glad that He loves you, my friend?

MALACHI 1:6-14

*A son honoreth his father, and a servant his master;
if, then, I be a father, where is mine honor? And
if I be a master, where is my fear? saith the LORD
of hosts unto you, O priests, that despise my name.
And ye say, In what way have we despised thy
name? Ye offer polluted bread upon mine altar;
and ye say, In what way have we polluted thee?
In that ye say, The table of the LORD is contemptible.
And if ye offer the blind for sacrifice, is it not
evil? And if ye offer the lame and sick, is it not
evil? Offer it now unto thy governor; will he be
pleased with thee, or accept thy person? saith the
LORD of hosts. And now, I pray you, beseech God
that he will be gracious unto us. This hath been
by your means; will he regard your persons? saith
the LORD of hosts. Who is there even among you
that would shut the doors for nothing? Neither
do ye kindle fire on mine altar for nothing. I have
no pleasure in you, saith the LORD of hosts, neither
will I accept an offering at your hand. For from
the rising of the sun even unto the going down
of the same, my name shall be great among the
nations, and in every place incense shall be offered
unto my name, and a pure offering; for my name
shall be great among the nations, saith the LORD
of hosts. But ye have profaned it, in that ye say,
The table of the LORD is polluted; and the fruit
of it, even its food, is contemptible. Ye said also,
Behold, what a weariness is it! And ye have sniffed*

at it, saith the LORD of hosts; and ye brought that which was torn, and the lame, and the sick; thus ye brought an offering. Should I accept this of your hand? saith the LORD. But cursed be the deceiver, who hath in his flock a male, and voweth, and sacrificeth unto the Lord a corrupt thing; for I am a great King, saith the LORD of hosts, and my name is terrible among the nations.

chapter 2

A COMPROMISING CLERGY

What was the highest office in Israel? The king? No. The highest office was the priesthood, for the priest was a mediator between God and man. It was the priest who offered the atoning sacrifice for sin and conveyed God's love, mercy, and blessing on the people. It was the priest who instructed the people in holiness, taught the Law, and functioned in Israel's high court as a judge.

The priest was consecrated to his office in an elaborate ceremony. His body was washed with water, blood atonement was offered on the altar for his sins, holy anointing oil was poured over him, and official garments draped his body for service.

The priests knew their awesome responsibility before the Lord. But by the time Malachi wrote his prophecy, they had desecrated their office, defamed God's name, and were held in disgrace by the people.

God's Sacredness Defamed

The relationship that God established with Israel from their inception as a nation was that of father and son (Ex. 4:22; Hos. 11:1). The Law commanded that a son honor his father (Ex. 20:12; Dt. 5:16) and a servant respect his master (v. 6). If Judah were both a son and a servant, God questioned, "where is mine honor? And if I be a master, where is my fear [respect]?" (v. 6).

The word *honor* comes from the Hebrew word *kabod*, which means *glory*. God was entitled to both honor and glory, but He received neither from Judah during this time. How ironic that the fathers of Judah demanded honor from their sons, in keeping with the Law, but they deliberately transgressed the Law when it came to honoring God. Even more ironic was that they despised (had contempt for) God's name. What an indictment of the priesthood. How true the words of Isaiah, "The ox knoweth his owner, and the ass, his master's crib, but Israel doth not know" (Isa. 1:3).

If the priests—who taught the Law, led in worship, and were to be an example to the people—despised God's name, how much more so would the people? Blind to their spiritual condition, the priests had the audacity to ask an unthinkable question: "In what way have we despised thy name?" (v. 6). The spiritually blind are often self-deceived and unaware of their guilt.

Often throughout the centuries this has been the case with Israel's spiritual leaders. Jesus, seeing the blindness of Israel's spiritual leaders, called them "blind leaders of the blind" (Mt. 15:14; 23:1-39). This condition will worsen during the Great Tribulation as multitudes are swept away by the deceptive lie of the Antichrist (2 Th. 2:9-11).

God's Sanctuary Desecrated

How had Israel despised God's name? First, they offered "polluted bread" (v. 7) on the altar. This does not refer to the showbread displayed in the Holy Place but, rather, to animal sacrifices that were considered bread to the Lord (Lev. 21:6; Ezek. 44:7).

These sacrifices could have been polluted in two ways. First, a defective, sick, or lame offering was strictly forbidden by the Law (Lev. 22:17-30). Israel had been warned that such sacrifices profaned God's name. They committed the very sin God had prohibited—not out of ignorance, for they knew the Law, but out of indifference to it. Second, the word *polluted* referred to priestly contamination, for they offered sacrifices without washing their hands or changing their clothes between offerings. This automatically disqualified them as unclean to perform their priestly functions. Therefore, the priests not only despised God's name but polluted everything their hands touched—the sacrifice, the altar, and their service to God.

Once again the priests had the audacity to question God's indictment against them: "In what way have we polluted thee?" (v. 7). Notice that they did not claim ignorance of the Law, pretending to be surprised that God had pronounced them guilty of defilement, but asked about the specific charge.

God's Sacrifice Defective

Another way in which the priests despised God's name was by saying, "The table of the LORD is contemptible" (v. 7). Again, this does not refer to the table of showbread but to the brazen altar where sacrificial animals were offered to the Lord. God specifically questioned the priests about their actions, inquiring whether they thought it wrong to offer "blind . . . lame and sick" (v. 8) animals on the altar. Their natural response should have been to condemn such offerings, but they gave no such answer.

In a sarcastic tone, Malachi questioned, "Offer it now unto thy governor; will he be pleased with thee, or accept thy person?" (v. 8). The prophet was urging the priests to take blind, crippled, and diseased animals to the governor and see if he would favorably accept them and their gifts. No credible priest would dare offer such worthless sacrifices to the governor. The governor would likely bring swift judgment against such an insult. How much more absurd it was to offer worthless gifts to God, who is the great Judge of the universe.

Contrast King David's attitude in acquiring Araunah's threshing floor to build an altar before the Lord. Araunah offered the floor to David free of charge, but David, showing character, said, "Nay, but I will surely buy it of thee at a price; neither will I offer burnt offerings unto the LORD my God of that which doth cost me nothing" (2 Sam. 24:24). Any service performed by a true servant of God costs something in time, money, and physical strength. It would be easy to criticize the actions of these priests, but many Christians offer God that which costs them nothing. Many lavish money on themselves but give little to God or His work. Many dress in the latest styles but give their castoffs to the missionaries. Many enjoy expensive vacations but will not provide airfare for a missionary to return to his field of service.

Malachi continued to urge the priests, "beseech God [soften Him up, or appease the face of God] that he will be gracious" (v. 9). The prophet was saying, *Since this has been your conduct, and this is the way you are bent on continuing, do not stop now. But do you really think God will show favor on and acceptance of such attitudes and actions? Never! A holy God cannot accept unholy or hypocritical service.*

For many in God's service, ministry has more show than substance, more getting for self than giving to others, more glorifying of self than of God. Their service seems empty, and they wonder why God is not blessing their work.

God's Servants Demeaning

The Temple worship had become degenerate and despicable. It would have been better to close it than to continue its contemptible service. Malachi asked, "Who is there even among you that would shut the doors . . . ?" (v. 10). He was hoping that a conscientious priest with spiritual character and conviction would step forward and close the Temple until the sinful practices were terminated. It was useless to "kindle fire" (v. 10).

The Priests' Actions

The priests were so corrupt that no one would step forward to "shut the doors for nothing" or "kindle fire . . . for nothing" (v. 10). They would not serve in the Temple without being paid up front for the most trivial services. Some were remiss in doing their duty even after receiving remuneration.

God would rather have seen the Temple closed than continue this hypocritical worship. In the past, He had become weary with corrupt worship and refused to accept sacrifices. Isaiah gave this account:

> To what purpose is the multitude of your sacrifices unto me? saith the LORD; I am full of the burnt offerings of rams, and the fat of fed beasts, and I delight not in the blood of bullocks, or of lambs, or of he-goats. When ye come to appear before me, who hath required this at your hand, to tread my courts? Bring no more vain oblations; incense is an abomination unto me; the new moons and sabbaths, the calling of assemblies, I cannot bear; it is iniquity, even the solemn meeting. Your new moons and your appointed feasts my soul hateth; they are a trouble unto me; I am weary of bearing them. And when ye spread forth your hands, I will hide mine eyes from you; yea, when ye make many prayers, I will not hear. Your hands are full of blood (Isa. 1:11-15).

God eventually allowed the Temple to be destroyed (586 B.C.). Even Jesus had to cleanse the Temple in His day and stated, "My house shall be called the house of prayer, but ye have made it a den of thieves" (Mt. 21:13). God again closed the Temple in 70 A.D., and it remains closed to this day.

Many churches, like the Temple, should be closed. This may seem like a harsh statement, but upon reflection it is a valid one. Many go through ritualistic litany and liturgy that have little meaning in their lives. The church at Laodicea was such a church, and God said, "I will spew thee out of my mouth" (Rev. 3:16). God closed not only the church at Laodicea but eventually all seven churches mentioned in Revelation 2 and 3.

God did not need Judah's worship, for He said, "from the rising of the sun even unto the going down of the same, my name shall be great among the nations" (v. 11). Scholars disagree on whether this verse should be interpreted in the present or future tense. Those interpreting the statement in the present tense show that the words "shall be" (v. 11) have been added by the translator. Thus, the verse would read, "My name is great among the nations." In that day, God's name was great among the nations, for many not only heard of but saw His mighty acts on behalf of Judah (v. 14; Dan. 6:25-27). But there is a problem if the verse is interpreted in the present tense, for how are the words "in every place incense shall be offered unto my name" (v. 11) to be taken? Do they refer to the Jews offering incense throughout the world? This would be impossible, because Jerusalem was the only place where offerings could be made. Neither could it refer to Jews from other nations bringing offerings to Jerusalem, for the Diaspora had not yet taken place. Nor can the verse refer to pagan Gentiles offering in their respective countries or Jerusalem. Therefore, this verse must refer to the future Kingdom age when God's name will be honored by a "pure offering" (v. 11) among the nations. At that time the nations will come to Jerusalem and worship the true God of Israel.

The King James Version seems to indicate that Gentiles will make offerings "in every place," but the preposition *in* can be translated *from*; thus, the verse could read "from every place" Gentiles will bring their offerings to be presented on the altar in Jerusalem. Today God's name is great among the nations, for He has called out a remnant who are proclaiming His praise throughout the world. During the Kingdom age, this witness will be even greater.

The Priests' Attitudes

Malachi dealt not only with the priests' actions but also with their attitudes about the polluted sacrifices: "But ye have profaned it, in that ye say, The table of the LORD is polluted; and the fruit of it, even its food, is contemptible" (v. 12). The priests showed no respect for either the Lord's table (altar) or its fruit (the meat offering). It is inevitable that those who despise the Lord's altar will defile it.

Godless Service Denounced

God's Charges Against the Priests

Malachi enumerated four charges that God had against the priests. First, they approached their ministry halfheartedly. "Ye said also, Behold, what a weariness is it!" (v. 13). Instead of viewing their ministry as a high and holy privilege, the priests saw it as boring and burdensome. Those who perform their ministry in the flesh will find it to be arduous, meaningless drudgery.

Paul was a superb example of one with a servant's attitude. He suffered every possible physical and mental discouragement and weariness known to the ministry, yet he was able to say, "For which cause we faint not; but though our outward man perish, yet the inward man is renewed day by day. For our light affliction, which is but for a moment, worketh for us a far more exceeding and eternal weight of glory" (2 Cor. 4:16-17). Paul's secret for enduring the struggles in God's service was to walk in the Holy Spirit's power with his eyes fixed on the Lord, not on himself or his circumstances. D. L. Moody said it succinctly: "I become weary *in* well doing, but not weary *of* well doing." How true of Paul and all servants who minister in God's power.

Second, they "sniffed at" their service before the Lord (v. 13). They turned up their noses in belittlement at serving in God's Temple, as one who turns away from obnoxious food. They considered their priestly duties to be a burden, a dull ritualistic routine performed mechanically with no care. Such service would become wearisome.

Third, the priests allowed people to bring sacrifices that were "torn . . . lame . . . sick" (v. 13), an act condemned by the Law. For the priests to offer such sacrifices was the epitome of spiritual debauchery. Again, the Lord asked, "Should I accept this of your hand?" (v. 13). Naturally not, for they were against God's revealed will and holy nature. Many are quick to condemn both priests and people, yet they too offer spiritual

31

service that costs them nothing. They rob God by giving halfhearted worship, offering tired minds and bodies for service, and spending little time preparing for the ministry they are called to perform.

Fourth, God pronounced a curse on those who made deceptive vows. They were tricksters who played games with God. They vowed to sacrifice an unblemished male animal on the altar, then substituted a blemished male or a female animal (less valuable) in its place (v. 14). This was strictly forbidden by the Law. Did the priests and people really think they could trick an omniscient God? If God's name was terrible (held in fear and dread) among unbelieving nations, how much more should Judah, who knew God's judgments, revere Him?

The Believer-Priest's Trust

Many Christians vow to serve the Lord during times of commitment but fail to present all that the vow demands. Solomon wrote, "When thou vowest a vow unto God, defer not to pay it; for he hath no pleasure in fools. Pay that which thou hast vowed. Better is it that thou shouldest not vow, than that thou shouldest vow and not pay" (Eccl. 5:4-5).

This point was illustrated dramatically at the inception of the Church. Ananias and Sapphira vowed to sell their land and give the money to the church. But they defrauded God by failing to give the total amount of the sale of their land. Swift judgment fell on both when they were confronted with their deception: They died immediately (Acts 5:1-11). Peter's words say it all: "Thou hast not lied unto men, but unto God" (Acts 5:4). How many have promised to tithe but cheat God every week? How many promise to pray for specific requests but never do? How many make commitments to pastors, missionaries, friends, or church boards and never fulfill their vows?

Jesus asks the believer-priest today a very important question: "why call ye me, Lord, Lord, and do not the things which I say?" (Lk. 6:46). There is a charge (trust) to keep when one claims Christ as Lord. Charles Wesley caught this vision while reading Matthew Henry's commentary on Leviticus 8:35. Henry wrote, "We shall everyone of us have a charge to keep, an eternal God to glorify, an immortal soul to provide for, one generation to serve." Inspired by Henry's words, Wesley wrote a hymn titled "Keep the Charge of the Lord That Ye Die Not." Later the hymn was retitled "A Charge to Keep I Have."[1] The first two stanzas go like this:

> A charge to keep I have,
> A God to glorify,
> A never-dying soul to save,
> And fit it for the sky.
>
> To serve this present age,
> My calling to fulfill;
> O may it all my powers engage,
> To do my Master's will!

Christian friend, are you honoring or dishonoring God's name? Remember, He is either Lord of all or Lord not at all!

ENDNOTES

[1] Kenneth W. Osbeck, *101 More Hymn Stories* (Grand Rapids: Kregel, 1985), p. 14.

MALACHI 2:1-9

And now, O ye priests, this commandment is for you. If ye will not hear, and if ye will not lay it to heart, to give glory unto my name, saith the LORD of hosts, I will even send a curse upon you, and I will curse your blessings; yea, I have cursed them already, because ye do not lay it to heart. Behold, I will corrupt your seed, and spread dung upon your faces, even the dung of your solemn feasts; and one shall take you away with it. And ye shall know that I have sent this commandment unto you, that my covenant might be with Levi, saith the LORD of hosts. My covenant was with him of life and peace; and I gave them to him for the fear with which he feared me, and was afraid before my name. The law of truth was in his mouth, and iniquity was not found in his lips; he walked with me in peace and equity, and did turn many away from iniquity. For the priest's lips should keep knowledge, and they should seek the law at his mouth; for he is the messenger of the LORD of hosts. But ye are departed out of the way; ye have caused many to stumble at the law; ye have corrupted the covenant of Levi, saith the LORD of hosts. Therefore have I also made you contemptible and base before all the people, according as ye have not kept my ways, but have been partial in the law.

chapter 3

THE PRIESTHOOD: GOD'S EKG OF ISRAEL

"Son, you must be disciplined for what you did!" The word *discipline* struck fear in the son's heart, as big tears poured from his eyes. He knew the punishment that awaited.

The same is true spiritually. God, like a father, must discipline His children who are disobedient to His Word. Spiritual leaders who blatantly defame and demean their call are especially accountable. Such was the case in Judah, for the priests had polluted everything they touched.

The Priests Cursed

Malachi's Indictment

Malachi pronounced a severe indictment against the priests because they had dishonored God's name (1:6-14). This indictment came in the form of a commandment (admonishment, v. 1) to turn from evil. If they took the warning to heart (v. 2), God would withhold judgment. But if they continued in the path of disobedience, He would send the curses prophesied against Israel as they entered Canaan (Dt.27:9-26; 28:15-68).

God's Judgments

Several judgments would befall the priests as a result of God's curse.

The first judgment was that God corrupted their seed (v. 3). Some believe this meant that God would curse fields, making them unproductive. This interpretation is doubtful, since the priests received most of their physical provisions from the people. Others teach that the word for *seed* (*zera*) should be translated *arm* (*zeroa*). The text would then read, "I will rebuke your arm" (v. 3), using the word *arm* as a metaphor for the priests' strength or ability in performing their priestly duties (*The Bible Knowledge Commentary* [Revell], Malachi, p. 1579). Still others believe it refers to the priests' offspring being removed from their official duties. This interpretation seems to best fit the context.

The second judgment was that God degraded the priests. He would spread dung (excrement) on their faces and solemn feasts (v. 3). The Law demanded that an animal's unclean organs and dung be burned outside of the city (Ex. 29:14). In this instance, God would mix together the parts of the sacrifice and rub the filth on the priests' faces. He used the most degrading terminology possible to describe what He thought of the priests and their service. Note that they are called "*your* solemn feasts." God would have no part in them.

Third, God removed the priests from their duties. The priesthood would suffer the same fate as the dung: "and one shall take you away with it" (v. 3). They would be removed from their priestly duties. Judah's priests should have taken this warning to heart, for they knew what had happened to King Jeroboam and King Jehoiakim. Jeroboam and his sons were taken away as refuse because he had done more evil than all who lived before him (1 Ki. 14:9-10). He and his dynasty were not buried after their deaths but remained on the ground (outside the city) to be devoured by wild beasts and birds. Jehoiakim suffered a similar fate after his death. He had the "burial of an ass, drawn and cast forth beyond the gates of Jerusalem" (Jer. 22:19). When an animal died in Jerusalem, its body was thrown over the city wall and left to decay or be devoured by beasts of prey. The unfaithful priests were to suffer a similar fate.

God did not want mere lip service from the priests. He wanted total life commitment. If they remained in their apathetic condition, the Lord would curse their blessings one by one.

In fact, God had "cursed them already" (v. 2), for He knew that the priests would not repent of their sin. The Lord desires more than lip service from believers today. He wants a life submitted to Him. The believer who hears God's Word but does not put its precepts into practice lives a life of self-deception:

> But be ye doers of the word and not hearers only, deceiving your own selves. For if any be a hearer of the word, and not a doer, he is like a man beholding his natural face in a mirror; For he beholdeth himself, and goeth his way, and immediately forgetteth what manner of man he was. But whosoever looketh into the perfect law of liberty, and continueth in it, he being not a forgetful hearer but a doer of the work, this man shall be blessed in his deed (Jas. 1:22-25).

The Priests' Covenant

The priests would experience the reality of God's discipline for two reasons: (1) so that they would know that God's commandments were not empty threats, and (2) so that His "covenant might be with Levi" (v. 4), meaning that the tribe of Levi would remain the official ministering body within the Temple. If God did not bring the priests to a place of repentance, He would, of necessity, have to destroy them for their sin.

The Priesthood's Provisions

Malachi reminded the priests of their lofty covenant relationship with God. God wanted the covenant made with the Levitical priesthood to provide "life and peace" (v. 5). They were to experience a life of spiritual peace and physical prosperity.

The covenant of life and peace was first bestowed on Phinehas for his stand against evil. Before Israel went into Canaan, Balaam tried to curse the nation, but he was unsuccessful. Because the curse did not work, he tried to corrupt the nation by having them worship Baal-peor and practice sexual immorality with Moabite women, a fertility practice associated with the worship of Baal. While Moses gave the pronouncement to have all those practicing these abominations destroyed, Zimri brought a Midianite prostitute named Cozbi into his tent and committed fornication with her (v. 6). Phinehas, Aaron's grandson, outraged by such a bold act, grabbed his javelin, entered Zimri's tent, and killed him and Cozbi. Because of his deed, God confirmed a "covenant of peace" on Phinehas and his descendants. Phinehas' deed turned away God's wrath from the people (Num. 25:1-15).

By mentioning the covenant of peace made with Phinehas, Malachi made several comparisons between the priests of his day and those of the past. Phinehas showed that he held God's name in reverential awe, but the priests of Malachi's day brought about God's wrath by their attitudes and actions (1:7-8, 12-14). Phinehas experienced peace and life during a very disruptive time, but these priests, although living in peace, would have peace and life taken away from them (vv. 2-3).

Today, life and peace are obtained through Jesus the Messiah. He secured them for all who put their faith in Him through His death on the cross. "But he was wounded for our transgressions, he was bruised for our iniquities; the chastisement for our peace was upon him, and with his stripes we are healed" (Isa. 53:5). "Therefore, being justified by faith, we have peace with God through our Lord Jesus Christ" (Rom. 5:1).

Those who truly walk in Christ's commandments will experience peace in a troubled world. As Jesus said, "Peace I leave with you, my peace I give unto you; not as the world giveth, give I unto you. Let not your heart be troubled, neither let it be afraid" (Jn. 14:27) and "These things I have spoken unto you, that in me ye might have peace. In the world ye shall have tribulation: but be of good cheer; I have overcome the world" (Jn. 16:33).

The Priesthood's Principles

The Levitical priesthood was led by principles: "The law of truth was in his mouth, and iniquity was not found in his lips" (v. 6). The "law" refers to the Mosaic Law, which the priests taught to the people (Dt. 33:8-11; Neh. 8:7-8), who in turn taught it to their children (Dt. 6:6-9). But the priests in Malachi's day were led by their own pernicious ways and not by the principles of God.

The believer who hides God's Word in his heart and meditates on its principles will find the secret to spiritual prosperity (Josh. 1:8).

The Priesthood's Prudence

The Levitical priesthood was prudent, "and iniquity was not found in his lips" (v. 6). The word *iniquity* means "unfair decision" (*The Pulpit Commentary*, vol. 14, Malachi, p. 20). The priest not only taught the Law but served as a judge and was expected to make fair judicial decisions between people (Dt. 17:8-9; 19:17-18). It stands to reason that if the priests in Malachi's day were corrupt and deceptive in their religious practices, they did not make proper judicial decisions (v. 9). During the Kingdom age, the Messiah will rule justly:

> And shall make him of quick understanding in the fear of the LORD; and he shall not judge after the sight of his eyes, neither reprove after the hearing of his ears, But with righteousness shall he judge the poor, and reprove with equity for the meek of the earth; and he shall smite the earth with the rod of his mouth, and with the breath of his lips shall he slay the wicked. And righteousness shall be the girdle of his loins, and faithfulness the girdle of his waist (Isa. 11:3-5).

The Priesthood's Practice

The Levitical priesthood practiced what it preached. God said, "he walked with me in peace and equity" (v. 6). Because the priest governed his conduct by God's Law, he lived a righteous life resulting in personal peace. The priests of Malachi's day, however, were derelict in their duty and could find no solace from God in times of chastening. True peace and righteousness come not only in knowing God's Word but in practicing its precepts.

The Priesthood's Prevention

The word and walk of the Levitical priesthood prevented sin by turning "many away from iniquity" (v. 6). Spiritual leaders have a tremendous impact on people for good or evil. They can turn people toward or away from God by their talk and walk. The priests of Malachi's day turned people *to* iniquity, not *away from* it.

The Priesthood's Preservation

The Levitical priesthood preserved the Law: "For the priest's lips should keep knowledge, and they should seek the law at his mouth" (v. 7). The word *keep* means to *guard* or to *preserve* the Law from perversion. It was the priest's duty to study the Law and then teach it to others. In Malachi's day, the priests perverted the Law by their words and teachings.

Today the believer should be eager to show that he is an approved workman for the Lord by diligently studying God's Word and rightly dividing it (2 Tim. 2:15). Only then is he prepared to preserve the Word of God from error and properly teach others.

The Priesthood's Proclamation

The Levitical priesthood proclaimed the Law: "for he is the messenger of the LORD of hosts" (v. 7). The priest both explained and exhorted or declared God's message to the people. This is the only place in Scripture where the priest is called the messenger of God. The priests in Malachi's day had no message to proclaim because sin had sealed their lips.

The believer is a messenger of Christ. As God's ambassador, he is not to represent himself but the Lord, who sends him throughout the world to proclaim the message of salvation to a lost humanity. The New Testament teaches this mandate:

Go ye, therefore, and teach all nations, baptizing them in the name of the Father, and of the Son, and of the Holy Spirit (Mt. 28:19).

But ye shall receive power, after the Holy Spirit is come upon you; and ye shall be witnesses unto me both in Jerusalem, and in all Judea, and in Samaria, and unto the uttermost part of the earth (Acts 1:8).

How, then, shall they call on him in whom they have not believed? And how shall they believe in him of whom they have not heard? And how shall they hear without a preacher?... So, then, faith cometh by hearing, and hearing by the word of God (Rom. 10:14, 17).

The Priests' Corruption

Malachi pointed out to the priests four ways in which they had broken their covenant relationship with God. They had "departed" (v. 8) from the prescribed obligations of their office. Their instruction was destructive. Instead of turning people away from iniquity, they caused them to "stumble at the law" (v. 8). They desecrated their covenant relationship with God by corrupting the "covenant of Levi" (v. 8). They were deceptive in their execution of justice. God told them, "ye have not kept my ways, but have been partial in the law" (v. 9). Perverting justice by showing respect of persons for selfish ends was a gross violation of the Law (Lev. 19:15).

How ironic that the people were warned not to depart from the priests' teachings, while the priests themselves had departed from those teachings. It was as if they were saying, "Do as I say, not as I do." Their own walk was not according to their word. Could God do any less than judge them?

The Christian must remember that, as a believer-priest, his works will be judged. Each believer will stand before the

Judgment Seat of Christ to give an account of his or her service in this life.

Three Kinds of Christian Workers
1. The Master Builder
2. The Shoddy Builder
3. The Destructive Worker

In 1 Corinthians 3:9-17, Paul presented three kinds of Christian workers: Master builders lay a solid foundation of good works, shoddy builders are careless and inept at their service, and destructive workers offer service that is destructive rather than constructive.

After a solid foundation is laid, different materials can be used for the superstructure. These include lasting materials like gold, silver, and precious stones, which endure the test of time, and faulty materials such as wood, hay, and stubble, which do not last. Every person's service will be tested by fire to see what kind of work it is. The combustible materials (symbolic of worthless service) are consumed immediately, leaving no trace of their substance. This kind of builder shall "suffer loss; but he himself shall be saved, yet as by fire" (1 Cor. 3:15). The loss suffered is only the believer's reward, not his salvation. The one whose works stand the test of fire will "receive a reward" (1 Cor. 3:14). The reward is not clarified, although praise will be a part of it (1 Cor. 4:5). The word *reward* comes from a Greek word that means *wage*. There is a payday coming for every believer. It is possible for a person to deceive other believers concerning his service, but God knows the true motive of every worker and work.

The apparent success of some ministries in the eyes of man does not mean that they have God's approval and blessing. Only the day of judgment will reveal the true quality of a ministry. Each believer who serves must make sure his life is clean, his motives are God-honoring, and his service is implemented in the power of God's Spirit.

The Priests Condemned

The priests were condemned for their corrupt practices. God allowed them to be viewed as "contemptible and base before all the people" (v. 9). Notice that they received the same judgment they had sown. The priests held God's table in contempt, and then the people held the priests in contempt. How true is God's Word: "Be not deceived, God is not mocked, for whatever a man soweth, that shall he also reap" (Gal. 6:7).

God's Discipline

No son likes to be disciplined by his father, but discipline is necessary to guide the son toward maturity. The father who does not administer discipline does not truly love his son.

God loves the believer as a son, and for this reason He disciplines him toward Christian maturity: "For whom the Lord loveth he chasteneth, and scourgeth every son whom he receiveth" (Heb. 12:6). The word *chasten* has the idea of *instructive discipline*, as one would use to train a child. Discipline is not meted out as punishment but is meant to instruct the individual in the way he should walk. The word *son* does not refer to a child but to an adult son, one who can very quickly understand God's instruction in his life and respond accordingly.

The Believer's Choice

The believer can avoid chastening by repenting the moment he sins. God said, "if we would judge ourselves, we should not be judged" (1 Cor. 11:31). The believer is given a choice: Through self-examination he can remove sin from his life, or he can wait until God does it through chastening. God disciplines the son back to a place of commitment so that he will "not be condemned with the world" (1 Cor. 11:32). Those who continually ignore the chastening of God may become physically weak or sick, or may even die (1 Cor. 11:30). Naturally, chastening is grievous and never joyous, but when it is over, it will yield the "peaceable fruit of righteousness" (Heb. 12:10-11) in a person's life. We can agree with V. Raymond Edman's statement, "In an undisciplined age when liberty and license have replaced law and loyalty, there is greater need than ever before that we be disciplined to be His disciples."[1]

ENDNOTES

[1] V. Raymond Edman, *The Disciplines of Life* (Wheaton: Van Kampen Press, 1948), p. 9.

MALACHI 2:10-16

Have we not all one father? Hath not one God created us? Why do we deal treacherously, every man against his brother, by profaning the covenant of our fathers? Judah hath dealt treacherously, and an abomination is committed in Israel and in Jerusalem; for Judah hath profaned the holiness of the LORD which he loved, and hath married the daughter of a foreign god. The LORD will cut off the man that doeth this, the master and the scholar, out of the tabernacles of Jacob, and him that offereth an offering unto the LORD of hosts. And this have ye done again, covering the altar of the LORD with tears, with weeping, and with crying out, insomuch that he regardeth not the offering any more, or receiveth it with good will at your hand. Yet ye say, Why? Because the LORD hath been witness between thee and the wife of thy youth, against whom thou hast dealt treacherously; yet is she thy companion, and the wife of thy covenant. And did not he make one? Yet had he the residue of the spirit. And why one? That he might seek a godly seed. Therefore, take heed to your spirit, and let none deal treacherously against the wife of his youth. For the LORD, the God of Israel, saith that he hateth putting away; for one covereth violence with his garment, saith the LORD of hosts; therefore, take heed to your spirit, that ye deal not treacherously.

chapter 4

THE BROKEN MARRIAGE COVENANT

The United States has the highest divorce rate in the world—almost 50 percent. Many more couples are emotionally divorced from each other and would like to terminate their marriages. They stay together because of economics, children, or religious belief. Amazingly, 85 percent of divorced people try marriage a second time within five years.

None of this is new. Twenty-five hundred years ago, divorce was a major problem in Judah. Men were divorcing the wives of their youth to marry foreign women. This practice was an abomination in God's sight. Thus, God called Malachi to speak out against the degrading practice that had emerged throughout the land.

Mixed Marriage Laws Violated

Previously the prophet had presented God's indictment and then waited for a counterclaim of innocence from the people. In this section, Malachi changed his approach and led up to the indictment by presenting three questions to the men of Judah.

Three Questions for Judah

"Have we not all one father?" (v. 10). Malachi was not referring to their father Abraham, but to God, for He is the original father of Judah.

"Hath not one God created us?" (v. 10). This question does not refer to the creation of all mankind but to the time when God forged Israel into a people. God had created Israel for Himself so that they could proclaim His praise throughout the world (Isa. 43:1, 7, 21). He considered Israel His "jewels"

(3:17), which means that they were a treasured possession, precious in His sight.

"Why do we deal treacherously, every man against his brother, by profaning the covenant of our fathers?" (v. 10). The word *treacherously* is used five times in this section (vv. 10, 11, 14, 15, 16) and means to deal *deceitfully* or *unfaithfully* with one another. The people were unfaithful in their relationships with God and with their family and friends.

Judah profaned the covenant of their fathers by marrying the "daughter of a foreign god" (v. 11). The word for *married* used in this passage is *baal*, the noun form of which means *lord, master, husband*. Notice the play on words: "married [*baal*] the daughter of a *foreign god*" (v. 11). Baal was the false god worshiped by the Canaanites and Phoenicians.

This was not the first time that Israel had committed sin with women who practiced Baal worship. Before Israel entered Canaan, Balaam had tried to corrupt the nation by getting the men to practice sexual immorality with the women of Moab, which led to the worship of Baal-peor (Num. 25:1-4).

Solomon was drawn into the same trap centuries later. God had warned him not to marry foreign women, for eventually they would turn away his heart after their gods (1 Ki. 11:2). But Solomon disobediently clung to these women in love. After his death, the kingdom was divided and later fell to the Babylonians.

God had strictly forbidden intermarriage by the Israelites to protect the nation from idolatry (Ex. 34:11-16; Dt. 7:3-4; Josh. 23:12-13). The nation's open disobedience of the marriage laws reflected their degree of disregard for their God, nation, and families. Malachi told Judah that their practice of mixed marriage was an "abomination" to God (v. 11), "a term reserved for the worst of evils, such as immorality, witchcraft, or idolatry."[1]

It has never been God's plan for believers to marry unbelievers. "Be ye not unequally yoked together with unbelievers," said the Apostle Paul (2 Cor. 6:14). The concept of being "unequally yoked" is taken from Deuteronomy 22:10, where the Israelites were told not to plow with an ox (a clean animal) and an ass (an unclean animal) yoked together. Their natures and temperaments made them incompatible and uncooperative for plowing. The same is true for a believer who tries to establish a harmonious walk through life with an unbelieving partner.

Five Rhetorical Questions for the Believer

Paul reinforced this principle by asking five rhetorical questions: "what fellowship [partnership] hath righteousness with unrighteousness? And what communion [things in common, fellowship] hath light with darkness? And what concord [harmony] hath Christ with Belial [Satan]? Or what part hath he that believeth with an infidel [unbeliever]? And what agreement [union] hath the temple of God with idols?" (2 Cor. 6:14-16). The answer to all of these questions is, None! Therefore, the believer is not to be yoked in an unholy relationship with an unbeliever, which would defile his or her relationship with Christ.

The Consequences of Judah's Actions

What was the consequence for marrying a foreign woman? "The LORD will cut off the man that doeth this, the master and the scholar, out of the tabernacles of Jacob" (v. 12). The words *master* and *scholar* are difficult to translate from the Hebrew text. The phrase has been translated, "everyone who awakes and answers" (NAS); "whoever he may" (NIV); or "anyone who gives testimony in behalf of the man who does this" (NIV margin). Whatever the exact translation, the meaning is clear. The man who committed such an act would be cut off, and possibly his family as well.

Believers do not realize the web they weave for themselves by marrying unbelievers. They often look back in deep sorrow over their actions, wishing they had thought twice before entering into such unholy relationships.

Those who married idolatrous women believed that God would forgive their sin if they brought the proper "offering unto the LORD" (v. 12). But they were wasting their time, for "The sacrifice of the wicked is an abomination to the LORD" (Prov. 15:8). Here we see the epitome of hypocrisy and insensitivity. This calls to mind the judgment that struck Eli. He and his family were cut off from the priesthood because he refused to discipline the wicked practices of his two sons regarding their Tabernacle service (1 Sam. 2:29-35).

Marriage Laws Violated

In the previous section, Malachi presented the sin and then the judgment that would follow. In this section he reversed the order, mentioning the judgment and then the sin.

Those presenting an offering covered "the altar of the LORD with tears" (v. 13). Some believe that these people were the priests, because they were the ones who offered sacrifice. Others believe them to be the divorced Israelite wives crying out for justice on the unjust acts of their husbands. Still others teach that these were men in general who cried out for mercy and forgiveness when God rejected their offering and worship. Most likely those in tears were both the priests and the men of Judah.

Completely baffled by God's rejection, the worshipers asked, "Why?" In no uncertain terms, Malachi pointedly gave them an answer: "Because the LORD hath been witness between thee and the wife of thy youth, against whom thou hast dealt treacherously; yet is she thy companion, and the wife of thy covenant" (v. 14). The answer is clear. God rejected their worship because they had broken the marriage covenant by divorcing their wives. The covenant they made in marriage was not only before human witnesses; it was also before God. Note the description God used of their marriages: "wife of thy youth . . . thy companion, and the wife of thy covenant."

Today many view marriage as a contract, not a covenant. If the contract does not work out, the parties involved mutually agree to terminate the agreement and go their separate ways, and a divorce ensues.

The Jewish Marriage

The Jewish marriage was not a contract but a "covenant" (v. 14; cp. Prov. 2:17). The major characteristic of a biblical marriage involved the parties obligating themselves to an unalterable and permanent relationship for life.

The Bible does not stipulate a marriageable age for either a man or woman, but in later Judaism marriage was permissible after the boy's bar mitzvah (13 years old) and the girl's coming of age (12 years old). Marriages were arranged by parents; thus, the individuals had little to say about whom they would marry. The betrothal was considered to be a binding agreement between the parents of the couple. If a man sexually abused a betrothed virgin, the Law demanded that he be stoned to death (Dt. 22:23-24).

The marriage agreement was made final when the groom paid the necessary bride price to the father of the bride. Then the marriage ceremony began with the bridegroom taking his bride from her house to his. The procession was preceded by a group of singing and dancing musicians. The bride knew the groom was coming for her when she heard the sound of the procession, and she eagerly awaited his arrival with her attendants. Upon taking his bride, the groom ushered the whole wedding party back to his father's house for the wedding feast. The feast and merriment lasted for a week or two. A marriage covenant (*ketuba*) was drawn up by the bride's father for the participants to sign. A bridal chamber (*huppa*), to which the veiled bride and groom were escorted, was made ready. There they consummated their marriage. The commitment was to be for life, and in God's eyes only death could terminate the marriage.

God's Plan for Marriage

Malachi reminded Judah of God's original plan for marriage: "And did not he make one?" (v. 15). The man and woman were to leave their fathers and mothers and become "one flesh" (Gen. 2:24). By creating man and woman, God was still left with the "residue of the spirit" (v. 15). His creative powers were not depleted in making Adam and Eve. He could have made more.

If God could have created more, then why only one pair? He had one purpose in creating the pair: "That he might seek [aim at] a godly seed" (v. 15); that is, a godly couple would produce godly children. God created man and woman for each other so that they could establish a stable home environment in which to rear godly children who would go out and do likewise.

Warning Against Infidelity

For this reason, man is to take heed and not "deal treacherously [unfaithfully] against the wife of his youth" (v. 15). To do this, the husband must put a guard over his eyes, heart, and motives so that he will not be tempted to leave the wife of his youth.

The temptation to infidelity is greater than ever before. The "new morality" has set standards in society that create an atmosphere conducive to infidelity. Businessmen spend more time with female associates than with their own wives. Career-minded women, in climbing the corporate ladder, feel they have outgrown their husbands, and a change must be made, or vice-versa. Travel jobs create adverse effects on marriage and set up opportunities for infidelity. The pressures of modern life cause spouses to look outside the home for someone who will listen, understand, or comfort them in a time of need. Soon a relationship develops that neither party anticipated. These are only some of the factors contributing to unfaithfulness in marriage and the high divorce rate today.

God's position on divorce is very clear: "he hateth putting away [divorce]" (v. 16). God hates divorce because it violates His original creative plan for marriage and brings untold hardships on those involved, destroying both the family and society.

Therefore shall a man leave his father and his mother, and shall cleave unto his wife; and they shall be one flesh (Gen. 2:24).

And he answered and said unto them, Have ye not read that he who made them at the beginning, made them male and female; And said, For this cause shall a man leave father and mother, and shall cleave to his wife, and they two shall be one flesh? Wherefore, they are no more two, but one flesh. What, therefore, God hath joined together, let not man put asunder (Mt. 19:4-6).

Why, then, did Moses make provision for husbands to divorce their wives? Jesus told the Pharisees that because of the hardness of their hearts, God allowed them to put away their wives; but divorce was never in God's plan for married people (Mt. 19:7-8). We must remember that Moses did not command divorce, but he established laws to regulate a permitted practice already in existence.

Divorce in Moses' day was much different than it is today. He permitted it for two reasons. First, so that the wife would have a document of protection; thus, society would know her true marital standing, which would guard against wife exchanging. Second, it prohibited a woman who had been divorced, remarried, and divorced again from remarrying her first spouse; this was forbidden by the Law.[2]

Malachi said that the person who divorced his wife "covereth violence with his garment" (v. 16). This figure of speech is better translated, "violence covereth" the man. As a man's garment tells much about him and covers his whole body, so it is with the man who divorces the wife of his youth to marry an idolatrous woman. He wears both his character and his sinful act for all to see.

Once again Malachi concluded with a warning to guard against unfaithfulness: "therefore, take heed to your spirit, that ye deal not treacherously" (v. 16). With the breakdown in marriage today, we cannot be reminded too often of the serious repercussions unfaithfulness brings.

The story is told of two children, a boy and a girl, who were fighting and screaming at one another. The concerned mother of the girl ran into the yard demanding an explanation for the commotion. "Oh, we weren't fighting; we were playing house. He's the father, and I'm the mother," replied the little girl. We might find this explanation amusing, but it is so true of many marriages today. Children mimic what they see their parents doing.

Maybe you, like the children in the story, have not taken your marriage seriously. You are only playing a game of husband and wife. Maybe you are weary of trying to hold together a fragile, faltering marriage. Maybe you are on the verge of divorcing the wife or husband of your youth to marry another. Whatever your situation, there is an answer if you are willing to seek it. Consult a pastor, counselor, or some other person who will help you through this difficult time. Remember, God hates divorce!

ENDNOTES

[1] Herbert Wolf, *Haggai and Malachi: Rededication and Renewal* (Chicago: Moody Press, 1976), p. 88.
[2] Walter C. Kaiser, Jr., *Malachi: God's Unchanging Love* (Grand Rapids: Baker Book House, 1984), p. 73.

Ye have wearied the LORD with your words. Yet ye say, In what way have we wearied him? When ye say, Every one that doeth evil is good in the sight of the LORD, and he delighteth in them; or, Where is the God of justice? Behold, I will send my messenger, and he shall prepare the way before me; and the Lord, whom ye seek, shall suddenly come to his temple, even the messenger of the covenant, whom ye delight in; behold, he shall come, saith the LORD of hosts. But who may abide the day of his coming? And who shall stand when he appeareth? For he is like a refiner's fire, and like fullers' soap. And he shall sit like a refiner and purifier of silver; and he shall purify the sons of Levi, and purge them like gold and silver, that they may offer unto the LORD an offering in righteousness. Then shall the offering of Judah and Jerusalem be pleasant unto the LORD, as in the days of old, and as in former years. And I will come near to you in judgment; and I will be a swift witness against the sorcerers, and against the adulterers, and against false swearers, and against those that oppress the hireling in his wages, the widow, and the fatherless, and that turn aside the sojourner from his right, and fear not me, saith the LORD of hosts. For I am the LORD, I change not; therefore ye sons of Jacob are not consumed.

chapter 5

WHERE IS THE GOD OF JUSTICE?

When Judah returned to her land, she expected to experience prosperity and glory, as in the days of Solomon. But this was not to be the case. In fact, she found just the opposite. Her wicked enemies lived in prosperity while Judah suffered privation. This caused the people to question whether God was truly holy and just.

Malachi warned Judah that God's patience was wearing thin, for he said, "Ye have wearied the LORD with your words." Once again Judah claimed to be ignorant of the charge against them and questioned, "In what way have we wearied him?" (2:17).

Judah's False Complaints

In Malachi 2:17, the prophet specified three false complaints Judah had uttered against God. First, "Every one that doeth evil is good in the sight of the LORD." The leaders reasoned that the Lord prospered the wicked and left His own righteous people in poverty; therefore, the wicked must be considered good in God's eyes. Second, "he delighteth in them." Not only did God prosper the wicked, but He took pleasure in doing so, said Judah. Third, they asked, "Where is the God of justice?" With sarcastic skepticism, they questioned whether God was even available to take just action against the wicked.

Judah questioned God because material prosperity, in the eyes of the Old Testament believer, was a sign of God's blessing to those who were obedient to Him. Others, such as Job, David, Solomon, Jeremiah, and Habakkuk, also were perplexed about God's blessing of the wicked. In the New Testament, God revealed that His blessings come to the just and the unjust alike (Mt. 5:45). Although the wicked do prosper, God's hand of judgment ultimately falls on them (Ps. 73:11-20; Hab. 2:3; 3:2-9).

Judah totally misunderstood the ways of God. He never winked at wickedness or took delight in the wicked, as Judah should have known from their past. The opposite is true, for "He that justifieth the wicked, and he that condemneth the just, even they both are an abomination to the LORD" (Prov. 17:15).

"Where is the God of justice?" Little did Judah know what they were asking. God responded to their question, but not in the way they expected, for the Lord executed judgment not only on the Gentiles but on sinners in Judah as well.

The Messenger's Preparation

Malachi stated that before the Lord appeared He would send His messenger to prepare the way (v. 1). Who is the messenger to whom Malachi referred? It is not an angel, although angels were used as messengers from God. There is no record that an angel brought a message to Israel before the Messiah appeared at the Temple. Neither is the messenger Malachi (although his name means *messenger*), for the message was not to be presented in his day. It would be given when the Messiah came to "his temple" (v. 1).

His Identity

The messenger would be one "who shall prepare the way before" the Messiah (v. 1; cp. Isa. 40:3). It is clear from the Gospels that John the Baptist fulfilled this prophecy when he announced the Lord's First Coming.

For this is he that was spoken of by the prophet, Isaiah, saying, The voice of one crying in the wilderness, Prepare ye the way of the Lord, make his paths straight (Mt. 3:3).

The voice of one crying in the wilderness, Prepare ye the way of the Lord, make his paths straight (Mk. 1:3).

As it is written in the book of the words of Isaiah, the prophet, saying, The voice of one crying in the wilderness, Prepare ye the way of the Lord, make his paths straight (Lk. 3:4).

He said, I am the voice of one crying in the wilderness, Make straight the way of the Lord, as said the prophet, Isaiah (Jn. 1:23).

Jesus confirmed that Malachi's prophecy was fulfilled in John the Baptist (Mt. 11:10). John was equated with Elijah as well, for he came in the spirit and power of the prophet (Mt. 11:14; 17:10-13; Lk. 1:17). Why, then, did John deny that he was the Elijah who was to come (Jn. 1:21)? Perhaps John denied being Elijah according to Jewish expectations in the first century.

His Mission

The priests were not only unprepared for the Messiah's coming in John's day, but they were putting in the way of the people spiritual stumbling blocks that John had to remove:

O generation of vipers, who hath warned you to flee from the wrath to come? Bring forth, therefore, fruits befitting repentance. And think not to say within yourselves, We have Abraham as our father; for I say unto you that God is able of these stones to raise up children unto Abraham. And now also the axe is laid unto the root of the trees; therefore, every tree which bringeth not forth good fruit is hewn down, and cast into the fire (Mt. 3:7-10).

In biblical times, it was customary to send men ahead when a great leader or king was coming to smooth the road, remove obstacles such as stumbling stones, and fill in ruts. The fact that John had to clear the way showed that people were spiritually unprepared for the Messiah's coming. Likewise, most people are not ready for His coming today.

Messiah's Presentation

Malachi shifted from speaking about the messenger to the coming of the Messiah. The words "before me . . . saith the LORD of hosts" (v. 1) indicate that God was speaking of the Messiah, for the "me" is connected with "LORD," "the messenger of the covenant" is the Messiah (God's Son), and the second "LORD" is God the Father, who is doing the speaking, showing a plurality in the Godhead.

Messiah's Coming Unexpected

The Messiah will "suddenly [unexpectedly] come to his temple" (v. 1). Jesus did appear unexpectedly at the Temple during His First Coming, when His parents dedicated Him (Lk. 2:21-38) and later when He cleansed it (Jn. 2:14-16; Mt. 21:12-13). But the word *sudden* appears "twenty-five times in the Old Testament, and in every case except one (2 Chr. 29:36), it is connected with disaster or judgment."[1] Therefore, this verse refers to the Messiah's Second Coming, called "the time of Jacob's trouble" (Jer. 30:7), when His judgment will fall on all unrighteous men.

Messiah: Messenger of the Covenant

The Messiah is called "the messenger [angel] of the covenant" (v. 1). Jesus Christ fulfilled this prophecy in several ways. First, He was involved with God the Father when He made several covenants with Israel, both unconditional (such as the Abrahamic Covenant) and conditional (as in the Mosaic Covenant). Second, He was the "angel of the LORD" who appeared to Israel in several Christophanies (Gen. 17:1; 18:1; Ex. 3:2; Jud. 13:6, 9). Third, he was the "angel of the LORD" who led Israel out of Egypt, protected them in the wilderness, and provided safe passage to the land of Canaan. Fourth, He is "the mediator of the new covenant" (Heb. 12:24; cp. Heb. 8:8-13).

Malachi reminded Judah that this coming Messiah is the one they "seek" and "delight in" (v. 1). The prophet may have meant this in one of three ways: (1) The Messiah they desired, sought, and hoped for would come; (2) they sought His coming to bring judgment on the Gentiles; or (3) in light of their sinful condition, Malachi spoke sarcastically to expose their real motive—they professed to seek the Lord while not truly desiring His coming.[2]

Many today profess that they are wanting, waiting, and watching for the Lord's return, but they really do not want Him to come until they finish living out the good life.

Messiah's Purging

The prophet asked two rhetorical questions about the Messiah's coming: "But who may abide the day of his coming? And who shall stand when he appeareth?" (v. 2). This prophecy combines aspects of Messiah's First and Second Comings but will find its ultimate fulfillment at His second advent, when He will judge the nations and the rebellious people of Israel. Who shall stand when He appears? No unrighteous person!

Fire and Soap

The illustrations of "fire" and "soap" (v. 2) describe what the Messiah's purging will be like when He comes in judgment. Fire is used to purge the dross from the metal. The "refiner [smelter] and purifier of . . . gold and silver" (v. 3) sits over a pot of molten metal, controlling the purifying process. He strains or filters out the dross until the metal is pure. When the metal becomes like a liquid mirror and he sees the reflected image of his face, the process is complete.

The fuller (laundryman) would take his soap (like lye or bleach), mix it with water, and scrub the cloth on a hard surface until the dirt was removed and the white garment glistened. Judah was so steeped in sin before their captivity (586 B.C.) that the lye and soap would not remove their iniquity. Even after their captivity, violence covered the garments of many in Judah.

God's purpose in cleansing the "sons of Levi" was to make them fit for service so that they could present their "offering in righteousness" (v. 3). Only then would "the offering of Judah and Jerusalem be pleasant [acceptable] unto the LORD, as in the days of old, and as in former years" (v. 4). Most likely "days" refers to the time of Moses and the United Kingdom period under David and Solomon. During the Millennial Kingdom, animal sacrifices will be offered in righteousness by Israel's priesthood, not for sin but as a memorial to the finished work of Christ's sacrificial death.

God's Judgments Upon People

Many judgments are mentioned in the Bible.

Judgment of the Believer's Sins: First is the judgment of the believer's sins, which occurred when Christ died on the cross. He has now been justified by putting his faith in Christ. "He that heareth my word, and believeth on him that sent me, hath everlasting life, and shall not come into judgment, but is passed from death unto life" (Jn. 5:24); "There is, therefore, now no condemnation to them who are in Christ Jesus, who walk not after the flesh, but after the Spirit" (Rom. 8:1).

Believer's Self-Judgment: The believer judges himself whenever there is known sin in his life—he confesses and forsakes the sin. "For if we would judge ourselves, we should not be judged" (1 Cor. 11:31).

Judgment of the Believer's Works: The believer's works, not sins (for they were judged on the cross), will be judged at the Bema judgment after the Rapture of the Church. "For we must all appear before the judgment seat of Christ, that everyone may receive the things done in his body, according to that he hath done, whether it be good or bad" (2 Cor. 5:10; cp. 1 Cor. 3:12-15).

God's Wrath Upon the Ungodly: During the Great Tribulation, God will pour out His wrath on the ungodly.

God's Judgment of the Jewish People: After His return to earth, the Messiah will regather the Jewish people from every land and take them into the wilderness, where He will purge all

68

rebels and unbelievers. Only the righteous of Israel will enter into the Kingdom: "As I live, saith the Lord GOD, surely with a mighty hand, and with an outstretched arm, and with fury poured out, will I rule over you; And I will bring you out from the peoples, and will gather you out of the countries in which ye are scattered, with a mighty hand, and with an outstretched arm, and with fury poured out" (Ezek. 20:33-34).

God's Judgment of the Gentile Nations: After His return, the Messiah will judge the Gentile nations. Only the righteous will enter into the Kingdom; the unsaved will be cast into everlasting fire. "And before him shall be gathered all the nations; and he shall separate them one from another, as a shepherd divideth his sheep from the goats . . . And these [goats] shall go away into everlasting punishment, but the righteous [sheep] into life eternal" (Mt. 25:32, 46; cp. vv. 33-45).

God's Judgment of the Wicked Angels: After the Millennial Kingdom, God will judge all wicked angels. "God spared not the angels that sinned, but cast them down to hell, and delivered them into chains of darkness, to be reserved unto judgment" (2 Pet. 2:4; cp. Jude 6; Rev. 20:10).

The Great White Throne Judgment: After the Kingdom age, a great white throne will be set up, and all people whose names are not written in the Book of Life will be judged and cast alive into the Lake of Fire (Rev. 20:11-15). All judgment has been given to Jesus the Messiah: "For the Father judgeth no man, but hath committed all judgment unto the Son" (Jn. 5:22).

All men experience the immutable law of sowing and reaping. Paul said, "Be not deceived, God is not mocked, for whatever a man soweth, that shall he also reap" (Gal. 6:7). The apostle urged us to stop our self-deception; we cannot fool God. If we continue to sow sin, God's judgment will fall on us, resulting in physical and spiritual destruction.

Messiah's Punishment

Malachi ushered the reader into God's courtroom. God, who is the great judge, is also the prosecuting attorney and key witness against Judah. He used three legal terms to present His indictment: "come near," "judgment," and "swift witness" (v. 5). God was about to answer Israel's question asked in Malachi 2:17. At times, judgment may seem to tarry, but when it falls, it will be swift.

God's Punishment Delayed

We are reminded of the scoffer's words, "Where is the promise of his coming? For since the fathers fell asleep, all things continue as they were from the beginning of the creation" (2 Pet. 3:4). The Lord is not slack concerning His coming. He will come. His seeming delay is the result of His love and long-suffering for sinners. He is "not willing that any should perish, but that all should come to repentance" (2 Pet. 3:9).

Sins That Bring Swift Judgment

Malachi named seven sins in four categories that bring swift judgment from God.

Sorcery: God will judge the "sorcerers" (v. 5) or those involved in witchcraft, a practice highly condemned under the Law and carrying a penalty of death (Ex. 22:18; Lev. 20:27; Dt. 18:9-14; Acts 8:9). Occultism is growing in the United States as many Oriental, philosophical, and religious systems have swept the country.

Adultery: God will judge "adulterers" (v. 5). The Ten Commandments strongly condemned this sin, but Judah continued to practice it. Adultery is running rampant in the United States as many practice premarital and extramarital sex.

Perjury: God will judge "false swearers" (v. 5). Those who committed perjury in a court of law were condemned under the Law of Israel (Ex. 20:7; Lev. 19:12; Dt. 19:16-20). Today lawsuits are at an all-time high in this country, with many people bringing false suits or, at best, claims only bordering on the truth.

Usery: God will judge those who defraud the defenseless in society—the employer oppressing "the hireling in his wages" (v. 5) or cheating the employee out of his pay. Such practices were condemned by Old Testament Law (Lev. 19:13; Dt. 24:15) as well as in the New Testament. "Behold, the hire of the laborers who have reaped down your fields, which is of you kept back by fraud, crieth; and the cries of them who have reaped are entered into the ears of the Lord of Sabaoth" (Jas. 5:4).

Three other groups are mentioned as being defrauded: "the widow, and the fatherless, and . . . the sojourner [alien]" (v. 5; Ex. 22:22-24; Lev. 19:10; Dt. 24:19-22; Zech. 7:10). In most cases, they are unable to defend themselves and are victimized by many who capitalize on their weak position. Those who commit such acts "fear not" the Lord (v. 5). Their lack of fear toward God is evident, for they show Him no respect nor do they have any relationship with Him. A true believer avoids such heinous acts.

Messiah's Preservation

God does not wink at wickedness or take delight in the wicked, as claimed by Judah. He said of Himself, "I change not" (v. 6). He is the unchangeable God who will not break His covenant relationship with Judah. For this reason, the "sons of Jacob are not consumed" (v. 6). Malachi called Judah "sons of Jacob" to remind them of their covenant relationship with God and to reemphasize His expressed love for them.

Although God may chasten Judah, they will not be consumed in judgment, for He will not break or take away His covenant promise to them. Although Israel sins, they will not lose their national hope of complete restoration (Rom. 11:25-29). The Jew's survival is guaranteed as long as the earth exists (Jer.31:35-37).

"Where is the God of justice?" This question is voiced by many when they hear of criminals being acquitted because

71

of legal technicalities or small fines being levied against large corporations who defraud people of millions of dollars. Remember, when we point a finger at others and ask, "Where is God's justice?" we are pointing three fingers at ourselves. If God were to pour out His justice on the world, where would we stand?

Be thankful that God, because of His love and long-suffering, has not rained down judgment on mankind. Be thankful that He is not willing for any to perish, but desires that all come to repentance. Be thankful that "It is because of the Lord's mercies [loving kindness] that we are not consumed" (Lam. 3:22). Be thankful that the God of justice appeared at His First Coming to provide for man's salvation.

Have you received salvation from the God of justice?

ENDNOTES

[1] Walter C. Kaiser, Jr., *Malachi: God's Unchanging Love* (Grand Rapids: Baker Book House, 1984), p. 84.

[2] Herbert Wolf, *Haggai and Malachi: Rededication and Renewal* (Chicago: Moody Press, 1976), p. 100.

MALACHI 3:7-12

Even from the days of your fathers ye are gone away from mine ordinances, and have not kept them. Return unto me, and I will return unto you, saith the LORD of hosts. But ye said, In what way shall we return? Will a man rob God? Yet ye have robbed me. But ye say, How have we robbed thee? In tithes and offerings. Ye are cursed with a curse; for ye have robbed me, even this whole nation. Bring all the tithes into the storehouse, that there may be food in mine house, and test me now herewith, saith the LORD of hosts, if I will not open for you the windows of heaven, and pour out for you a blessing, that there shall not be room enough to receive it. And I will rebuke the devourer for your sakes, and he shall not destroy the fruits of your ground; neither shall your vine cast its fruit before the time in the field, saith the LORD of hosts. And all nations shall call you blessed; for ye shall be a delightsome land, saith the LORD of hosts.

chapter 6

ROBBING A RIGHTEOUS GOD

With the exception of organized crime, robbery is the most prevalent and costly crime in America. Many are surprised to learn that shoplifting and employee theft rank together as the number one robbery category. Although most thefts involve less than $30.00 worth of goods, they account for 70 percent of the loss suffered by businesses and cost $24 billion annually.[1]

Shocked at such alarming statistics, many Christians are calling upon the court system to take strong measures to stem the crime wave sweeping this country. Yet, these same people might be shocked at how God views their lives when it comes to the subject of robbery.

The average Protestant is robbing God. He gives only three percent of his income to the church and one-tenth of one percent of his income—less than $3.00 annually per person— to missions. More money is spent on the care and feeding of pets than is given to churches and charities in the United States.

Malachi leveled the charge of robbery against Judah because they had cheated God in the area of giving. This practice brought a scathing reprimand from the prophet and a call for the nation to return to the biblical principle of tithing.

Return to God

Judah had failed to learn from their past. Their history was checkered with disobedience from the time of Moses. "Even from the days of your fathers ye are gone away from mine ordinances" was the Lord's indictment (v. 7). Yet, in a spirit of love, God stretched forth His hand and beckoned Judah to be reconciled to Him. "Return to me, and I will return to you" was His gracious invitation (v. 7). All Judah had to do was return and repent, and God would stay His hand of judgment and restore them to full blessing.

But sin had blinded the priests and people to their true spiritual condition. With a calloused lack of conscience, Judah claimed ignorance and innocence of any wrongdoing. The question "In what way shall we return?" indicated their attitude (v. 7).

Many believers today react in the same way when confronted with their standing before God. Sin has so lulled people into a spiritual stupor that they are robbed of any discernment about their true spiritual condition.

Robbing God

God pointed out Judah's sin by answering their question with another question. "Will a man rob God? Yet ye have robbed me" (v. 8). The Hebrew word for *rob*, which occurs only one other time in Scripture (Prov. 22:22), means to *defraud*. The verb has been used often in Talmudic literature and means "to take forcibly."[2]

Withholding from God and Others

How could mere, finite mortals rob the infinite God who created, sustains, sovereignly owns, and controls all things? They did it in several ways that have already been presented: by failing to honor God, by offering corrupt sacrifices and service in their worship, by breaking the covenant of marriage, and by defrauding the helpless. They robbed God by taking or holding back that which belonged to Him and others.

Once again Judah asked, "How have we robbed thee?" God's answer was succinct: "In tithes and offerings" (v. 8).

Tithes and Offerings

Israel was required by the Levitical Law to give tithes and offerings to God. First, they were to bring a tenth of all produce and livestock, or the financial equivalent, into the Temple for distribution among the Levites. The Levites, in turn, gave a portion of their tithe to the priests. Second, they brought another tithe to the Temple during special feast days. Every third year the second tithe was held within the hometown to be distributed among sojourners, the fatherless, and widows. Failure to tithe every three years defrauded these groups of their due. Third, all people over 20 years of age were required to pay a half shekel whenever a census was taken.

Failure to tithe properly could have included not paying the tithe at all, withholding part of it, or not giving it at the proper time. Whatever the reason, refusing to tithe according to the Law brought a curse: "Ye are cursed with a curse; for ye have robbed me, even this whole nation" (v. 9).

This is the third curse pronounced in the Book of Malachi thus far. First, the individual was cursed for the deceptive practice of offering corrupt sacrifices. Second, the priesthood was cursed for hypocritical service. Third, the nation was cursed for robbing God by failing to give their tithe. Notice that failure to tithe cut off blessings not only to the individual but to his family, neighbors, and the nation. Often Christians ask, "Why does God bless some with abundance and not others?" Although the ultimate reason is unknown, God does promise to pour out abundant blessing on those who are liberal givers. Those who rob God in their giving are actually robbing themselves.

Rewarding the Godly

The people would not be cursed if they obeyed the Lord. In fact, seeming disaster could be turned into blessing if they were faithful in their giving. The key to blessing was complete obedience: "Bring *all* the tithes into the storehouse" (v. 10).

The Principle of Tithing

The "storehouse" was the chamber in the Temple where the tithes and offerings were kept. Two things should be mentioned concerning the word *storehouse*. First, the word in context does not refer to the local church, for the church was not in existence during this time. Christians, however, should bring their gifts to the local church where they fellowship to support that ministry. Second, Scripture does not forbid giving to parachurch ministries. The issue is not dealt with because parachurch ministries were nonexistent at that time.

The question of Christian tithing has been debated through the centuries. There are two positions commonly held on the subject, and regardless of how the question is answered, objections are raised by the opposing position.

Some believe that tithing is to be practiced by Christians today for the following reasons: Tithing preceded the Law and was practiced by Abraham ("And blessed be the most high God, who hath delivered thine enemies into thy hand. And he gave him tithes of all," Gen. 14:20) and Jacob ("And this stone, which I have set for a pillar, shall be God's house: and of all that thou shalt give me I will surely give the tenth unto thee," Gen. 28:22). During His ministry, Jesus neither spoke against nor abolished the practice of tithing. In fact, He endorsed it. He told the Scribes and Pharisees, "For ye pay tithe of mint and anise and cummin, and have omitted the weightier matters of the law, justice, mercy, and faith; these ought ye to have done, and not to leave the other undone" (Mt. 23:23). In the epistles, no writer spoke against or did away with the principle of tithing. Therefore, it should be practiced today as a fair percentage required by God in support of His work. But giving should not be limited to the tithe, for free-will offerings are to be brought in addition to the tithe.

Others believe that the principle of tithing is not binding on the Christian today for the following reasons: The Bible did not institute tithing before the Law, for there is no record that Abraham and Jacob were instructed by God to tithe. It was an amount that they freely determined. Although the Israelite was required by Law to tithe, the principle is not binding on the Christian today, for he is not under the Mosaic Law. It is true that Jesus supported the tithe principle because

He was speaking in the context of the Law to those who were under the Law at that time, but He would not endorse it for those in the Church today. Although the writers of the epistles did not renounce the tithe, neither did they endorse it.

The Principles of Giving

The principles of New Testament teaching on giving are clearly presented in the Pauline epistles. "Upon the first day of the week let every one of you lay by him in store, as God hath prospered him, that there be no gatherings when I come" (1 Cor. 16:2; cp. 2 Cor. 8:2, 7-9, 12, 19-20; 9:5-12).

According to the Scriptures, giving must come from a willing heart, a right mental attitude, and on the basis of grace—not Law. The Christian is to lay up systematically a proportionate amount, as God has prospered him, and bring that gift to church on Sunday. Giving is to be voluntary out of what a person has and is proof of his sincere love for God. We are to count it a privilege to give sacrificially and liberally to God and His work. Giving is to be done by every one in the church, with no exceptions. Men of impeccable character are to be given oversight in the church. God will reward the faithful giver with joy, abundance if he sows liberally, and the ability to give even more.

Nowhere does Scripture teach that God's work is to be supported by unbelievers, financial gimmickry, church raffles, rummage sales, bake sales, car washes, coercion by church leaders, or special stewardship organizations called in to collect annual pledges from parishioners. These kinds of fund raising seem inconsistent with the grace-giving principles outlined above.

It may be good to start with the tithe as a proper standard for giving, but both Testaments teach that giving is not to be limited to this amount. The Israelite was required to bring his tithe along with offerings. It has been said, "If tithes and offerings were required under Law, how much more should the believer give under grace?" In fact, some who give only

10 to 20 percent of their annual income could actually be robbing God if their income is in the six- or seven-digit category.

God Rewards Faithful Giving

God challenged Judah to "test" (v. 10) or try His faithfulness in rewarding them for paying "all" the tithe that was required. If they were obedient, a number of blessings would be forthcoming.

Prosperity: God would rain prosperity on them: "I will . . . open for you the windows of heaven, and pour out for you a blessing" (v. 10). In other words, God would unlock His storehouse in Heaven if they filled His storehouse on earth. Then the Lord would send such an abundance of rain "that there shall not be room enough to receive it" (v. 10). This phrase literally means "until a failure of sufficiency."[3] Malachi challenged believers to try to exhaust God with giving. Naturally, this is impossible, for God has limitless resources. The promise of abundant rain was a blessing linked to an obedient walk by the nation: "The LORD shall open unto thee his good treasure, the heaven to give the rain unto thy land in its season, and to bless all the work of thine hand; and thou shalt lend unto many nations, and thou shalt not borrow" (Dt. 28:12).

He makes the same kind of promise to believers today. "But seek ye first the kingdom of God, and his righteousness, and all these things shall be added unto you" (Mt. 6:33). God gives proportionately to a believer's giving. "He who soweth sparingly shall reap also sparingly; and he who soweth bountifully shall reap also bountifully" (2 Cor. 9:6).

Pestilence Removed: "And I will rebuke the devourer for your sakes, and he shall not destroy the fruits of your ground" (v. 11). The devourer is any predator who would destroy their crops. The word *devour* means to *eat* or *consume,* and it was the name given to the locusts that swarmed over the fields in the Middle East, leaving nothing green in their path (Joel 1-2).

Renewed Productivity: God would renew productivity to the land: "neither shall your vine cast its fruit before the time in the field, saith the LORD of hosts" (v. 11). The word *cast* means to *miscarry* or *drop* the grapes before they have ripened. Obedience in the area of tithing meant a guaranteed harvest for Judah.

Restored Prominence: God would restore prominence to Judah in the eyes of other nations. "And all nations shall call you blessed" (v. 12). This will ultimately take place during the millennial reign of Christ. The restored Israel will become a blessing among the nations, be reestablished as the head of all nations, and receive worldwide acceptance: "And their seed shall be known among the nations, and their offspring among the peoples; all who see them shall acknowledge them, that they are the seed whom the LORD hath blessed" (Isa. 61:9).

In that day Israel will be a "delightsome land" (v. 12), one that is pleasurable and pleasing in which to dwell: "Thou shalt no more be termed Forsaken, neither shall thy land any more be termed Desolate; but thou shalt be called Hephzibah, and thy land Beulah; for the LORD delighteth in thee, and thy land shall be married" (Isa. 62:4). All nations will serve Israel in that day: "For the nation and kingdom that will not serve thee shall perish; yea, those nations shall be utterly wasted" (Isa. 60:12).

The Christian and Giving

Christians present many reasons and excuses for not giving to the Lord. Some have been taught improperly or not at all concerning what God requires in the area of giving. Some do not give out of greed and a desire to spend all their money on self-gratification. Some believe that they cannot afford to give because they have a young family to support, they are in debt, they are saving for retirement, they are on a pension, or they are simply too poor. Still others believe that because they are giving their lives to a full-time ministry, they are not required to give financially. The Scripture teaches that "every one" (1 Cor. 16:2) is required to give to the Lord's work. Those holding any of the above positions must restructure their giving according to biblical principles.

Christians cannot afford *not* to give. By robbing God of what is due Him, people actually rob themselves and their families of many personal blessings, for giving pays earthly and heavenly dividends:

> Give, and it shall be given unto you; good measure, pressed down, and shaken together, and running over, shall men give into your bosom. For with the same measure that ye measure it shall be measured to you again (Lk. 6:38).

> Lay not up for yourselves treasures upon earth, where moth and rust doth corrupt, and where thieves break through and steal, But lay up for yourselves treasures in heaven, where neither moth nor rust doth corrupt, and where thieves do not break through nor steal (Mt. 6:19-20).

How the Christian handles money is a true barometer of his spiritual life. The rich young ruler came to the awful realization that his wealth robbed him of eternal life because he put it before a personal commitment to Christ. "Jesus said unto him, If thou wilt be perfect, go and sell what thou hast, and give to the poor, and thou shalt have treasure in heaven; and come and follow me" (Mt. 19:21). Failure to handle money properly can rob Christians of spiritual growth, opportunities, and blessings. The Lord said, "If, therefore, ye have not been faithful in the unrighteous money, who will commit to your trust the true riches?" (Lk. 16:11).

Jesus did not mince words when He spoke about giving. He said, "For where your treasure is, there will your heart be also . . . No man can serve two masters . . . Ye cannot serve God and money" (Mt. 6:21, 24).

Have you taken a spiritual audit of your giving lately? Are you robbing God, like the average Protestant, by giving only three percent or less to the Lord? Are your treasures here on earth or in Heaven? Remember, "It is more blessed to give than to receive" (Acts 20:35)—in more ways than one. "How have we robbed you, God?" This is a question we must all ask ourselves.

ENDNOTES

[1] Youth Problems, Editorial Records Reports, "Shoplifting" (Washington, DC: Congressional Quarterly, 1982), p. 103.

[2] Joyce Baldwin, *Haggai, Zechariah, and Malachi* (Downers Grove, IL: Inter-Varsity, 1972), pp. 245-46.

[3] Walter C. Kaiser, Jr., *Malachi: God's Unchanging Love* (Grand Rapids: Baker Book House, 1984), p. 91.

MALACHI 3:13-18

Your words have been stout against me, saith the LORD. *Yet ye say, What have we spoken so much against thee? Ye have said, It is vain to serve God; and what profit is it that we have kept his ordinance, and that we have walked mournfully before the* LORD *of hosts? And now we call the proud happy; yea, they that work wickedness are set up; yea, they that test God are even delivered. Then they that feared the* LORD *spoke often one to another; and the* LORD *hearkened, and heard it, and a book of remembrance was written before him for them that feared the* LORD, *and that thought upon his name. And they shall be mine, saith the* LORD *of hosts, in that day when I make up my jewels; and I will spare them, as a man spareth his own son that serveth him. Then shall ye return, and discern between the righteous and the wicked, between him that serveth God and him that serveth not.*

chapter 7

THE TWO FACES OF JUDAH

A deceitful person is called two-faced or a hypocrite. *Hypocrite* was a word used in the Greek theater to describe an actor who put a large, painted mask in front of his face to denote the character he was playing, thus hiding his real identity.

This aptly described the priests of Judah who, like Greek actors, masked the truth about their commitment by putting on the face of innocence when the Lord charged them with corrupt worship and service. Such a facade wearied the Lord. Their words wearied Him as well, for they claimed that He delighted in their enemies by allowing them to prosper while His own people suffered affliction and privation. Such was not the case, but this attitude had filtered down to the people as well. They criticized God in the same way as their spiritual leaders did.

God had to address these arrogant accusations, especially after He had proposed to pour out a tremendous blessing on Judah if they were obedient in the area of giving.

Godless Rhetoric Reproved

"Your words have been stout [strong, overpowering] against me, saith the LORD" (v. 13). Instead of being humbled by God's charge, they reacted in the same sarcastic way as before. "What have we spoken so much against thee?" (v. 13), they questioned. *We do not remember saying anything against You, God!* Outraged by their response, God stripped away their arrogant mask of hypocrisy. He then used their own questions to pinpoint three ways in which they had spoken against Him.

Judah's Accusations

"It is vain to serve God" (v. 14). They saw their service as vain or empty, lacking any personal fulfillment. Although this was true in their case and testified to their bankrupt souls, their assessment was utterly false. In fact, the opposite is true. The only service that brings satisfaction in life is serving God in sincerity and truth.

"Ye have said . . . what profit is it that we have kept his ordinance?" (v. 14). Either the people had become self-deceived, blind to their spiritual condition, or they actually thought that they had fulfilled their religious obligations as set forth in the Law. Whatever the case, their assessment was untrue, for they had knowingly broken all of God's laws.

"Ye have said . . . what profit is it that we . . . have walked mournfully before the LORD of hosts?" (v. 14). Although the people had fasted in sackcloth and mourned over personal and national sins, their fasting was only a facade to mask their true spiritual condition. In other words, they were saying, *God, we have fulfilled the Law by carrying out our obligations, but You have not fulfilled Your promises to bless us.* Thus, their service had been without "profit" (v. 14). The word *profit* is a technical term used for a weaver cutting a piece of cloth free from the loom. Its use in Malachi had the negative connotation of men expecting their cut or percentage, as a racketeer or gangster would demand for evil work.[1]

This same attitude spilled over to the first century and aptly described many (but not all) Pharisees who postured an outward form of obedience to God but lacked obedience from the heart. Jesus warned that this kind of commitment flows from a heart filled with hypocrisy, for these people "say, and do not" (Mt. 23:3).

Many in the church are like the Israelites. They present the face of outward commitment to the Lord but have no commitment in their hearts. Their true motive for serving is profit, whether it be popularity, position, financial gain, or ego satisfaction.

Many religious telecasts present such an image. Some evangelists promise great profits (health, wealth, and success) to those who follow their faith formulas. They claim their wealth and success to be a testimony to God's touch and blessing on their lives, and they assure their viewers that they can have the same blessing from the Lord. Although they claim to be totally committed to the Lord, the discerning viewer is left with the impression that it is all a show to mask the profits they are gleaning.

Judah's Conclusions

The murmurers in Judah came to certain conclusions about their service, which actually mocked and contradicted what God had promised in verses 10 to 12. Their first conclusion was that the arrogant pagans were blessed by God: "we call the proud happy" (v. 15); that is, the truly blessed are not the faithful believers who serve God but the rebellious pagans who flaunt their opposition to God and oppress the righteous (cp. Habakkuk's similar complaint). This was contrary to what God had just said in verse 11. The opposite is true. He "rebuked the proud who are cursed" (Ps. 119:21).

Judah's second conclusion was, "they that work wickedness are set up" (v. 15). In other words, those who live in wickedness are actually built up or established with prosperity and wealth and are strongly rooted in their society. Again, this contradicts what God said in verse 10. Those who ultimately prosper are obedient in their giving and service to God.

The people finally concluded that those who "test God are even delivered" (v. 15). They believed that those who worked wickedness could provoke God into judging them because of their rebellion to His Law and that they would escape any punishment. Once again, this is a contradiction of God's Word, for He challenged the people to test Him and see if He would bless those who kept His commands.

God's Reproof

It may seem that those who test God escape His wrath, but Scripture teaches otherwise. Judgment will fall on the ungodly. Herbert Wolf presents a classic illustration of this truth from Israel's own history. During their 40 years of wilderness wandering, Israel continually murmured against God, putting Him to the test by demanding food and water: "And they tested God in their heart by asking food according to their desire . . . And he rained down manna upon them to eat, and had given them of the grain of heaven" (Ps. 78:18, 24; cp. Ex. 16:3; 17:2).

Their rebellious testing did not go unpunished; the whole generation eventually perished in the wilderness. At the time, it may have seemed that they escaped punishment, but that was not the case.[2] Judah's conclusion was based on viewing only their present situation and not on the ultimate result of the actions of arrogant unbelievers.

Often Christians think the way Judah did. They watch family members and friends verbally deny God, live wicked lives, and receive greater blessing than believers. To them, denying God seems to pay big dividends as they watch these people accumulate wealth, receive promotions, and buy bigger houses in better neighborhoods. Although they may not verbalize it, they cynically think, *What profit is there in serving God?* We must remember that God keeps the records, and payday will come in His good time. Ultimately, blessing will come to all who faithfully serve God.

Godly Remnant Remembered

There was another group of people in Judah whose commitment was not masked with hypocrisy. They are referred to as those who "feared the LORD" (v. 16). The phrase *fear the LORD* means to hold God in *awe and reverence* for who He is. It means to recognize God as the "beginning of knowledge"

(Prov. 1:7)—that is, the foundation or starting point of a life that pleases Him.

They Feared the Lord

This was not a fear based on feeling but was the result of hearing, learning, and responding to who God is from His Word. Those who feared God would keep His commandments, walk in righteousness, and put aside anything that would hinder worship and service to Him. This demanded total commitment of heart, soul, and body. When Solomon dedicated the Temple, he prayed that not only Israel but "all people of the earth" would fear the Lord (1 Ki. 8:43).

Those who feared the Lord received wisdom from God, which brought blessing and favor. The Book of Proverbs reveals much about the benefits God's wisdom provides.

> The fear of the LORD is the beginning of knowledge, but fools despise wisdom and instruction . . . Because they hated knowledge, and did not choose the fear of the LORD (1:7, 29).
>
> Then shalt thou understand the fear of the LORD, and find the knowledge of God (2:5).
>
> The fear of the LORD is to hate evil; pride, and arrogance, and the evil way, and the perverse mouth, do I hate (8:13).
>
> The fear of the LORD is the instruction of wisdom; and before honor is humility (15:33).
>
> He that walketh in his uprightness feareth the LORD, but he that is perverse in his ways despiseth him (14:2).
>
> The house of the wicked shall be overthrown, but the tabernacle of the upright shall flourish . . . The backslider in heart shall be filled with his own ways, and a good man shall be satisfied from himself (14:11, 14).
>
> The fear of the LORD prolongeth days, but the years of the wicked shall be shortened (10:27).
>
> In the fear of the LORD is strong confidence, and his children shall have a place of refuge (14:26).

The fear of the LORD tendeth to life, and he who hath it shall abide satisfied; he shall not be visited with evil (19:23).

They received wisdom from God, enabling them to walk in righteousness, that they might avoid evil. This, in most cases, produced longevity and satisfaction in life. Walking in the fear of the Lord was the key to receiving blessing and favor from God during that time, something that most of the priests and people of Judah had failed to do.

The Old Testament is replete with accounts of men and women who served God out of a healthy fear. Abraham offered Isaac on the altar of sacrifice out of a godly fear. Israelite midwives obeyed God by sparing the lives of male children because they feared the Lord rather than the king. Job testified that he feared God: "There was a man in the land of Uz, whose name was Job; and that man was perfect and upright, and one that feared God, and shunned evil . . . And the LORD said unto Satan, Hast thou considered my servant, Job, that there is none like him in the earth, a perfect and an upright man, one who feareth God, and shunneth evil?" (Job 1:1, 8). What a stark contrast to the priests of Malachi's day, who had no fear of the Lord.

God Remembered Their Words and Deeds

God took note of the Godfearers. He saw their continual fellowship with one another, for they "spoke often one to another" (v. 16). Those who are spiritually alive will seek out others of like commitment with whom to fellowship. He saw that they meditated on the things of God, for they "thought upon his name" (v. 16). The faithful remnant fixed their minds on God. How different their attitude was compared to that of the priests who despised God's name and looked on His table with contempt.

God "heard" and "hearkened" (listened) to their speech and was pleased (v. 16). The words of the wicked had "wearied" the Lord (2:17), for they were "stout" (v. 13) against

Him, but the words of the righteous remnant pleased Him. God recorded their words and deeds in a "book of remembrance" to be kept before Him (v. 16). This book is not the same as the "book of life" (Rev. 20:12, 15). God keeps books of man's deeds, whether they are good or bad: "And I saw the dead, small and great, stand before God, and the books were opened; and another book was opened, which is the book of life. And the dead were judged out of those things which were written in the books, according to their works" (Rev. 20:12; cp. Dan. 12:1).

He knew the righteous in Judah and kept an accurate record of their sufferings and trials in staying true to their commitment. David knew that God even kept a record of the tears he shed in times of trouble: "Depart from me, all ye workers of iniquity; for the LORD hath heard the voice of my weeping" (Ps. 6:8).

Man's tongue will eventually reveal what is in his heart, for out of the "abundance of the heart his mouth speaketh" (Lk. 6:45). In the day of judgment, man must give an account of every idle word he speaks: "But I say unto you that every idle word that men shall speak, they shall give account of it in the day of judgment" (Mt. 12:36). Many believers live as if God is deaf to their conversation and blind to their actions, but He catches and records every word and deed:

> For the word of God is living, and powerful, and sharper than any two-edged sword, piercing even to the dividing asunder of soul and spirit, and of the joints and marrow, and is a discerner of the thoughts and intents of the heart. Neither is there any creature that is not manifest in his sight, but all things are naked and opened unto the eyes of him with whom we have to do (Heb. 4:12-13).

God Treasured Them

Those who fear the Lord have a special relationship with Him; they are called His "jewels" (v. 17) or *treasured possession.*

These Godfearers are more precious than gold, silver, or the whole of the Lord's creation.

Israel became God's treasured possession when they entered into a covenant relationship with Him at Mount Sinai. The privilege was not unique to Israel, for all believers are "people of his own" (1 Pet. 2:9) treasured by the Lord.

God Protected Them

In addition to being God's possession, Israel also received God's protection "as a man spareth his own son that serveth him" (v. 17). This is true of the Christian who has been adopted into God's family as an adult son. He too is assured of His protection and care. The Lord has compassion on all those who fear Him, just as an earthly father does his children: "If ye then, being evil, know how to give good gifts unto your children, how much more shall your Father, who is in heaven, give good things to them that ask him?" (Mt. 7:11). God spares and blesses the righteous because they are His sons and serve Him in righteousness.

God said He would spare them "in that day" (v. 17)—the day of the Messiah's coming, when He will pour out judgment on the ungodly and blessing on the righteous. During the Great Tribulation, God will spare a faithful remnant from Israel and bring them safely into His kingdom.

When the Lord returns, Israel will be given convincing proof of God's moral government over this world and will be able to "discern between the righteous and the wicked" (v. 18). The crass accusations made by most in Judah—that God favors and blesses the wicked—will be proven false, for in that day God will bring swift judgment on all the wicked. The righteous remnant will see that He does reward those who faithfully fear and serve Him. The testimony on the lips of the righteous will be, "Verily, there is a reward for the righteous; verily, he is a God that judgeth in the earth" (Ps. 58:11).

Hypocrisy takes various forms and can subtly overcome the Christian who does not guard against it. The hypocrite postures the attitude and appearance of commitment, but inwardly he lacks sincerity and true piety and sometimes lives in sin. Others, although committed to the Lord, hypocritically judge the small faults in the lives of fellow Christians while refusing to acknowledge glaring sins in their own lives. "Thou hypocrite, first cast the beam out of thine own eye, and then shalt thou see clearly to cast the mote out of thy brother's eye" (Mt. 7:5). Still others hypocritically profess Christ as Savior but actually have never received Him.

Is there hypocrisy in your life? The question can be quickly settled by asking yourself, *Am I an actor, pretending to live a dedicated life before the Lord while in reality thinking and living the opposite?* Only you can answer this question and make the needed changes in your life.

ENDNOTES

[1] Walter C. Kaiser, Jr., *Malachi: God's Unchanging Love* (Grand Rapids: Baker Book House, 1984), p. 98.
[2] Herbert Wolf, *Haggai, Malachi: Rededication and Renewal* (Chicago: Moody Press, 1976), p. 114.

MALACHI 4:1-6

For, behold, the day cometh, that shall burn like an oven, and all the proud, yea, and all that do wickedly, shall be stubble; and the day that cometh shall burn them up, saith the LORD of hosts, that it shall leave them neither root nor branch. But unto you that fear my name shall the Sun of righteousness arise with healing in his wings; and ye shall go forth, and grow up like calves of the stall. And ye shall tread down the wicked; for they shall be ashes under the soles of your feet in the day that I shall do this, saith the LORD of hosts. Remember the law of Moses, my servant, which I commanded unto him in Horeb for all Israel, with the statutes and ordinances. Behold, I will send you Elijah, the prophet, before the coming of the great and terrible day of the LORD; And he shall turn the heart of the fathers to the children, and the heart of the children to their fathers, lest I come and smite the earth with a curse.

chapter 8

THE DAY OF THE LORD UNVEILED

Judah asked the question, "Where is the God of justice?"
With sarcastic skepticism, the nation was questioning
whether God was even available to take just action against
the wicked and provide justice for the righteous. In answer
to Judah's question, Malachi whisked the nation down the
corridor of time to unveil the great and terrible "day of the
LORD," a time when God will bring terrifying destruction on
the wicked and triumphant deliverance to the righteous. It
will be a day of judgment not only on Israel's enemies, but
on the wicked of the nation as well. For this reason, Malachi
made a final appeal for Judah to repent of their sin and be
reconciled to God.

The Wicked Eliminated

Malachi assured Judah that severe judgment would come
upon the wicked: "behold, the day cometh, that shall burn
like an oven" (v. 1). This "day of the LORD" will be a time
when God directly intervenes in the affairs of man. It will take
place after the Rapture of the Church and will cover the time
of the Tribulation, concluding with the Great White Throne
Judgment.

This judgment is described as a burning "oven" that will
destroy the wicked like dry stubble (v. 1). The judgment will
be so complete that "neither root nor branch" will be left (v.
1). This is not teaching the annihilation of the wicked, for they
will be resurrected to stand before the Great White Throne
Judgment.

> And I saw a great white throne, and him that sat on
> it, from whose face the earth and the heaven fled away,

and there was found no place for them. And I saw the dead, small and great, stand before God, and the books were opened; and another book was opened, which is the book of life. And the dead were judged out of those things which were written in the books, according to their works (Rev. 20:11-12; cp. Dan. 12:2).

After the wicked are judged, they will be cast into the Lake of Fire to suffer conscious torment forever: "And death and hades were cast into the lake of fire. This is the second death. And whosoever was not found written in the book of life was cast into the lake of fire" (Rev. 20:14-15; cp. 14:10-11).

The Worthy Exalted

The "Sun of Righteousness"

God promised to deliver the righteous in the "day of the LORD." Those who fear His name (hold it in reverence) will have the "Sun of righteousness" arise on them "with healing in his wings" (v. 2). When the Lord returns, His brightness will destroy the wicked but bring light and life to the righteous: "And then shall that wicked one be revealed, whom the Lord shall consume with the spirit of his mouth, and shall destroy with the brightness of his coming" (2 Th. 2:8). Light is like a laser: It can be used to destroy or heal.

Does the phrase *Sun of righteousness* refer to God the Father, Christ at His Second Coming, or simply righteousness shining forth like the sun during the Kingdom age? The metaphor applies to all three. The righteousness of both God the Father and Jesus Christ the Son will shine on the believer during the Kingdom age. Christ, who is called the "day star" (2 Pet. 1:19) and the "bright and morning star" (Rev. 22:16), will shine on the righteous as an everlasting light (Isa. 60:2, 19-20).

Christ's Ministry of Healing

The effects of Christ's ministry will be twofold. First, He will bring spiritual and physical healing for those who enter the Kingdom:

> And I will pour upon the house of David, and upon the inhabitants of Jerusalem, the Spirit of grace and of supplications; and they shall look upon me whom they have pierced, and they shall mourn for him, as one mourneth for his only son, and shall be in bitterness for him, as one that is in bitterness for his firstborn (Zech. 12:10).

> Then the eyes of the blind shall be opened, and the ears of the deaf shall be unstopped. Then shall the lame man leap as an hart, and the tongue of the dumb sing; for in the wilderness shall waters break out, and streams in the desert (Isa. 35:5-6).

Second, His glory will beam throughout the whole earth, permeating it with righteousness. "But with righteousness shall he judge the poor, and reprove with equity for the meek of the earth; and he shall smite the earth with the rod of his mouth, and with the breath of his lips shall he slay the wicked. And righteousness shall be the girdle of his loins, and faithfulness the girdle of his waist" (Isa. 11:4-5). This will result in the righteous going forth "like calves of the stall" (v. 2). They will become fat as a young calf who is driven from his stall to romp in the field and feast on the lush green pasture provided for his growth and satisfaction.

This righteous remnant, strengthened and encouraged by the Lord's return, will fight with Him to destroy the enemies of Judah. The wicked will become, as it were, ashes under the armies gathered against Jerusalem; their flesh will be consumed while they stand ready to fight the Lord: "and this shall be the plague with which the LORD will smite all the peoples that have fought against Jerusalem: their flesh shall consume away while they stand upon their feet, and their eyes shall consume away in their holes, and their tongue shall consume away in their mouth" (Zech. 14:12; cp. v. 2).

In that day God will silence the critics who claimed He prospered the wicked and ignored the privation of Judah, for the wicked will be dashed "in pieces like a potter's vessel" (Ps. 2:9) and mashed as if they had been put through a winepress:

> Who is this that cometh from Edom, with dyed garments from Bozrah? This that is glorious in his apparel, traveling in the greatness of his strength? I who speak in righteousness, mighty to save. Why art thou red in thine apparel, and thy garments like him who treadeth in the winefat? I have trodden the winepress alone, and of the peoples there was none with me; for I will tread them in mine anger, and trample them in my fury; and their blood shall be sprinkled upon my garments, and I will stain all my raiment. For the day of vengeance is in mine heart, and the year of my redeemed is come. And I looked, and there was none to help; and I wondered that there was none to uphold. Therefore, mine own arm brought salvation unto me, and my fury, it upheld me. And I will tread down the peoples in mine anger, and make them drunk in my fury, and I will bring down their strength to the earth (Isa. 63:1-6).

The Worthy Exhorted

In the final paragraph, Malachi admonished Judah to remember God's Law, which had been given on Mount Horeb in power and glory. The Israelites were to heed the statutes (ordinances) in their religious life and the judgments that governed their social life, for it was the Law that would keep Israel in a right relationship with God.

This reminder is important for several reasons. First, the Law expressed God's will for the people. Second, not just any law was to be followed, but only that given by Moses. Third, they were commanded to remember the Law, which meant they were not only to reflect on what they had learned but to live the principles they had learned as well. Fourth, the message was needed because Judah had ignored the Mosaic Law. Fifth, it would be another 400 years before God would speak to Judah—not until John the Baptist broke the silence did the nation hear from Heaven again. Sixth, unless the nation heeded the message, they would not escape the wrath of God's judgment.

So often believers take a mental trip when the pastor admonishes them to remember and apply the principles of Scripture to their lives. This is unfortunate, for only by recalling the principles and applying them to their lives are people able to live in submission to God's will.

The Work of Elijah

Malachi declared that God would send "Elijah, the prophet, before the coming of the great and terrible day of the LORD" (v. 5). Who is this Elijah?

Elijah's Identity

Some want to link Malachi 4:5 with 3:1 to teach that both prophecies were fulfilled in the person of John the Baptist. They argue that the language of these passages links them ("Behold," "I will send," "Prepare the way," and "He shall turn the heart") and that both prophecies are followed by the Lord's return.

Although John the Baptist prepared the way for Jesus (3:1; Isa. 40:3; Mt. 3:1-3), he said, "I am not [Elijah]" (Jn. 1:21). True, Jesus claimed that John the Baptist was the Elijah who should come, but He qualified His remarks with "if ye will receive it, this is Elijah, who was to come" (Mt. 11:14). Jesus was saying that if the Jewish people had received John's message, they would have received Him as the Messiah; thus, John would have fulfilled the Elijah prophecy in Malachi 4:5. But because Israel rejected Jesus' Messiahship, this prophecy awaits future fulfillment.

John the Baptist cannot be the fulfillment of Malachi 4:5 because after John's death, Jesus acknowledged that Elijah the prophet must come to restore all things before His return (Mt. 17:11). John the Baptist did not restore all things at His coming; thus, another prophet is yet to come in the spirit of Elijah.

Others do not look for a literal Elijah but for another prophet who will come in the spirit of Elijah. They hold this position for the following reasons: First, when Jesus said, "Elijah is come already, and they knew him not" (Mt. 17:12), He was not referring to a literal Elijah but to John the Baptist, who came in the spirit and power of Elijah. Second, if a literal Elijah had appeared before Jesus offered the kingdom to Israel, then Jesus did not offer the Kingdom, for Elijah did not come. But this was not the case. Jesus did offer the Kingdom to Israel; thus, the reference is not to a literal Elijah but to another prophet yet to come in the spirit and power of Elijah.

Still others hold that Elijah must personally come to prepare the way for Christ's Second Coming, as stated in Malachi 4:5 and Matthew 17:11. There is support for this position. First, Rabbinic Judaism teaches that Elijah will come personally (not just in spirit and power) before the Messiah's coming. Tradition teaches that He is recording the good works of the righteous to speed the day of Israel's redemption. In the "day of the LORD," He will overthrow the wicked nations who have persecuted Israel and also bring about the resurrection of the dead.

The hope is that Elijah will come during Passover. A place is prepared at the seder table with a large cup of wine (Elijah's cup) at his place setting. The front door is opened to welcome the spirit of the prophet. If Elijah were to visit the home, then the Jewish family would know that the Messiah's coming is very near.

Second, Jesus confirmed that Elijah must first come to "restore all things" (Mt. 17:11). Third, the two witnesses in Revelation 11 have a similar ministry to that of Moses and Elijah. The witnesses are described as prophets who are able to prevent rain from falling, turn water to blood, and hurt the earth with plagues, as did Moses and Elijah. Fourth, Moses and Elijah are mentioned together in both Malachi 4:4-6 and the Mount of Transfiguration passage (Mt. 17:3). Fifth, Elijah did not suffer physical death during his life; thus, he could very easily return as one of the witnesses to experience death.

Scripture teaches that Elijah must return "before the coming of the great and terrible day of the LORD" (v. 5), when God will pour out unprecedented wrath on the earth. If these days were not shortened, no human life would survive. "For then shall be great tribulation, such as was not since the beginning of the world to this time, no, nor ever shall be. And except those days should be shortened, there should no flesh be saved; but for the elect's sake those days shall be shortened" (Mt. 24:21-22).

Elijah's Ministry of Reconciliation

The coming Elijah is to have a ministry of reconciliation, resulting in a turning of "the heart of the fathers to the children, and the heart of the children to their fathers" (v. 6). This will take place when the two witnesses preach the gospel of the Kingdom during the Tribulation. Many unbelieving Jews will repent of their sins and be reconciled to God and family. They will again embrace the faith of Abraham, Isaac, Jacob, Moses, and the prophets. This reconciliation will prepare Israel for restoration when the Messiah returns. Although these believers will escape the wrath of God, many will suffer from the wrath of man during this time. The Antichrist will try to destroy them because they will not worship him (Rev. 6:9-11; 7:9-14).

Earlier Malachi confronted Judah with the same ministry of reconciliation, when God said to them, "Return unto me, and I will return unto you" (3:7). The words *return* and *turn* come from the same Hebrew word that means to *restore*. In his day, Malachi had hoped that the children (Judah) would return to the faith of their fathers, Abraham, Isaac, and Jacob. There is no indication that they ever did.

Failure to heed God's warning would result in the earth being smitten with a curse (v. 6). The word *curse* is different from the one previously used (2:2; 3:9). It means to *ban* or to *set apart under a ban* for utter extermination. A person, city, or thing could be put under the curse. All the cities destroyed by Joshua were cursed as well (Dt. 13:12-15).

If repentance were not forthcoming, Judah would be put under a curse—set apart for extermination. Malachi 4:6 was fulfilled in 70 A.D., when the Romans destroyed Jerusalem and Judah ceased to exist as a nation. The same curse will be experienced by the nations when Christ destroys them at His Second Coming. "And out of his mouth goeth a sharp sword, that with it he should smite the nations, and he shall rule them with a rod of iron; and he treadeth the winepress of the fierceness and wrath of Almighty God" (Rev. 19:15; cp. Mal. 4:3).

Because the Book of Malachi ends with a curse, the Jewish people repeat verse 5 after reading verse 6, so that the last words on their lips will not be a curse on their people. The same is done when reading Isaiah, Lamentations, and Ecclesiastes.

The curse was placed at the end of the book for a reason: People usually remember the last thing they read. The Jewish people were to remember that their refusal to obey God's will would result in judgment. But they could be delivered from the curse by repenting of their sin and being reconciled to God.

A Modern Perspective

Today man lives under the curse of sin and can be delivered from God's judgment only through Jesus the Messiah. Jesus, "the son of David, the son of Abraham" (Mt. 1:1), was made a curse for man to deliver him from the curse of sin. By His crucifixion on the tree, Christ redeemed both Jew and Gentile from the curse of the Law so that the blessing of salvation might be experienced by all who receive Him as Messiah. "Christ hath redeemed us from the curse of the law, being made a curse for us; for it is written, Cursed is everyone that hangeth on a tree; That the blessing of Abraham might come on the Gentiles through Jesus Christ, that we might receive the promise of the Spirit through faith" (Gal. 3:13-14).

The people of Judah had spurned God's love, despised His name, desecrated His Temple, defiled their marriages, and defrauded Him in their giving. They deserved to be cursed and destroyed. But, as the Old Testament drew to a close, God still expressed His love for Judah and, with an outstretched hand, beckoned the nation to come back to a place of forgiveness and fellowship.

Lest we think that this description is true solely of Judah, we need only look at the Church today or, in fact, at our own lives. So much of what has been said about Judah can be said about Christians. We must be reminded that God is keeping "a book of remembrance" (3:16) of each believer's works. After studying the indictment against Judah, how does your record measure up in God's book? Have you spurned God's love? Desecrated His house of worship? Defiled your marriage? Defrauded Him in giving? You too can repent of your sin and come to a place of forgiveness.

Throughout the Book of Malachi, God was searching for people who would unreservedly worship and serve Him. I am reminded of the words Henry Varley spoke to D. L. Moody in 1872, "The world has yet to see what God can do *with* and *for* and *through* and *in* a man who is *fully* and *wholly* consecrated to Him." Moody responded, "By God's grace, I want to be that man!"

As the day of the Lord's unveiling draws near, are you willing to be a man or woman God can use?

chapter 9

TRUTHS TO LIVE BY

The writer of Romans has so aptly stated, "For whatever things were written in earlier times were written for our learning, that we, through patience and comfort of the scriptures, might have hope" (Rom. 15:4). This encouragement means that past truth revealed through the Old Testament is profitable for the believer today.

Scripture is profitable in four ways. Through reading and studying the Scriptures, we *learn* about the past failures and victories of those who have gone on before us. This provides insight into how God dealt with His people in Old Testament times. Such lessons strengthen the believer and help produce *patience* (endurance) and *comfort* (encouragement and consolation) in times of trial. The believer will take *hope* (confidence) that his life is not being lived in vain. He will come to realize that God is in control; all things are working together in the believer's life for His glory.

Let's review some applications from earlier chapters that will help focus our faith toward a more fulfilling walk with the Lord.

God's Love

God's love for His people Israel is evident through this prophecy. The Lord loves not only Israel but the Church as well. A major reason God chose Israel and the Church was to manifest His love and praise throughout the world.

Like Israel, Christians with ungrateful hearts all too often are blind to the love and blessings of God. Some question God's love during times of extended trial or loss. No matter what trying experience the Christian must endure, the Lord still loves him.

Spiritual Discernment

The religious leadership of Israel lacked spiritual discernment. Their self-deception made them unaware that they had not honored or respected God in their daily walk and service. The same can be said of some Christians who slip into carnality. Because of their blindness, they are unable to discern how far they have drifted from their commitment to Christ.

Service for God

Ambassadors in Service

The priests were God's ambassadors to the people. They were required to teach the principles of the Law and to speak prudently on judicial matters among the people. They were to preserve the Law from perversion, explain what the Law meant, and proclaim and practice what they preached. But the priests were deceptive and derelict in their duty, blatantly defaming and demeaning their call to the priesthood even after being admonished often. Such deceit is called hypocrisy.

The Christian is an ambassador of Christ, called to represent God before an ungodly world. He should be eager to show himself as an approved workman for the Lord by giving diligent study to God's Word. As God's ambassador, he is to represent not himself but the Lord, who sends him throughout the world to proclaim the message of salvation to a lost humanity.

There are those who, like the priests, present the outward face of commitment to the Lord, but their hearts are not committed. Their true motive for serving is popularity, position, or profit. Some religious telecasters posture such an image. They present the face of total commitment to the Lord, but their "commitment" is only a mask for the profits they are gleaning. Secular correspondents have done in-depth research on such ministries and have documented their hypocritical nature.

Attitude in Service

The priests approached their service halfheartedly, seeing it as a boring, burdensome ritual. They scoffed at the privilege of serving in God's Temple, performing their duties in an insincere manner.

Christians often react in the same way. They go through the motions of serving God by halfheartedly offering tired minds and bodies and spending little time preparing for the ministry they vowed to perform. Jesus asks the believer-priest an important question: "why call ye me, Lord, Lord, and do not the things which I say?" (Lk. 6:46).

Action in Service

The priests offered defective sacrifices that, in turn, desecrated the Temple of God. To offer such sacrifices to the Lord was the height of hypocrisy.

It is easy to criticize the actions of these priests, but the offerings of many Christians today are also worthless. Many lavish money on themselves but give little to God or His work. Many dress in the latest styles but give only their castoffs to missionary endeavors. Others enjoy expensive vacations but will not provide airfare for a missionary to return to his field of service. For many in full-time service, ministry has more show than substance, more getting for self than giving to others, more glorifying of self than of God. There is a hollow ring to their words. Such ministry is devoid of God's blessing.

Accountability in Service

The priests in Israel will one day stand in judgment and be held accountable for disobedience in their duties. Christians must also remember that, as believer-priests, their works will be judged. All must stand before the Judgment Seat of Christ and give an account of their service in this life.

God loves the believer as a son, and for this reason He disciplines him toward Christian maturity. For the Christian, discipline is meted out not as punishment but, rather, to instruct

113

him in the way he should walk before God. The believer is given a choice. Through self-examination, he can remove sin from his life and avoid God's chastening. Those who choose to ignore the chastening may become weak or sickly, or even experience premature death. Chastening is often grievous and is never joyous; but once it is over, it yields the "peaceable fruit of righteousness" (Heb. 12:10-11).

The Marriage Relationship

The Marriage Covenant

The Jewish marriage was not a contract but a covenant. Malachi reminded Judah that God's original plan was for one man and one woman to be united in marriage. Biblical marriages require the two parties to obligate themselves to an unalterable and permanent relationship for the duration of their natural lives.

Today many see marriage as a contract rather than a covenant. If the contract does not work out, the parties involved mutually agree to terminate the agreement, go their separate ways, and obtain a divorce. This was never God's plan for His people, whether Jew or Gentile.

Mixed Marriages Condemned

God had strictly prohibited intermarriage by the Israelites to protect their nation from idolatry. Judah's practice of mixed marriage was an "abomination" to God, a term reserved for the worst of evils, such as immorality, witchcraft, and idolatry.

It has never been God's plan for believers to marry unbelievers. The concept of being "unequally yoked" comes from Deuteronomy 22:10, where the Israelite was not to plow with an ox (a clean animal) and an ass (an unclean animal) yoked together. The natures and temperaments of the two animals made them incompatible and uncooperative for plowing. The same is true of the believer who tries to establish a harmonious walk through life with an unbelieving partner.

People do not realize the web they weave for themselves by marrying unbelievers. Often they look back in sorrow, regretting that they entered into such an unholy relationship.

Marriage Commitment

The men of Judah were dealing "treacherously" (unfaithfully) with the wives of their youth (2:15); that is, they were divorcing them to marry foreign women. God's position on divorce is very clear: "He hateth putting away [divorce]" (2:16). God hates divorce because it violates His original creative plan for marriage and brings untold hardship for those involved, destroying both the family and, ultimately, society.

Why, then, did God allow Moses to make provision for men to divorce their wives? Jesus told the Pharisees that because of their hardness of heart, God allowed them to put away their wives. But divorce was never in God's plan for married people. We must remember that Moses did not *command* divorce; he set up laws to regulate divorce or *permitted* practices already in existence. With the breakdown in marriage today, we must realize the serious repercussions unfaithfulness brings.

Giving to God

Robbing God

Malachi accused Judah of robbing God in their "tithes and offerings" (3:8). This could have been done by not paying the tithe at all, withholding part of it, or not giving it at the proper time. Whatever the reason, refusing to tithe according to the Law brought a curse: "Ye are cursed with a curse; for ye have robbed me" (3:9).

The question of Christian tithing has been debated through the centuries. No matter how the question is answered, objections are raised by the opposing viewpoint. Some believe that the principle is not binding on the Christian in this age of grace.

The Scriptural teaching on Christian giving is as follows:
1. Giving must come from a willing heart and a right mental attitude.
2. Giving is based on grace, not Law.
3. The believer is to lay up systematically a determined amount, as he has been prospered, and bring it as a gift to church on Sunday.
4. Giving must be voluntary out of what the individual possesses and is proof of his love for God.
5. The believer is to count it a privilege to give sacrificially and liberally to the Lord's work.
6. All in the church, from the pulpit to the pew, are expected to give financially to the Lord's work.
7. Men of impeccable character are to be given oversight in collecting, counting, and caring for the gifts donated to the local church.
8. God will reward the faithful giver with joy, abundance if he sows liberally, and the ability to give even more.
9. Nowhere does Scripture teach that God's work is to be supported by unbelievers, financial gimmickry, church raffles, special sales, car washes, or special pledges. These principles are inconsistent with the grace-giving principles outlined above.

It would be good to start with the tithe as a proper standard for giving, but both Testaments teach that giving is not to be limited to a tithe.

Rewards from God

God challenged Judah to test or try His faithfulness in rewarding them for paying all the tithe that was required. He makes the same kind of promise to the believer today. "But seek ye first the kingdom of God, and his righteousness, and all these things shall be added unto you" (Mt. 6:33). God gives proportionately to the believer's giving. "He who soweth sparingly shall reap also sparingly; and he who soweth bountifully shall reap also bountifully" (2 Cor. 9:6).

By robbing God of what is due Him, people are actually robbing themselves and their families of many personal blessings and heavenly dividends. Jesus did not mince words when He spoke about the believer's attitude toward giving. He said, "For where your treasure is, there will your heart be also . . . No man can serve two masters . . . Ye cannot serve God and money" (Mt. 6:21, 24).

Often Christians ask why God blesses some with abundance and not others. Although the ultimate reason is unknown, God does promise to pour out abundant blessings on those who are liberal givers.

Remembering the Righteous

The Old Testament is replete with men and women who served God out of a healthy fear. God took note of the Godfearers. They are called His "jewels" or treasured possessions. These Godfearers are more precious than gold, silver, or the whole of the Lord's creation. God watched over the righteous in Israel and protected them "as a man spareth his own son that serveth him" (3:17).

This is true also of the Christian, who is a treasured possession of the Lord. He has been adopted into God's family as an adult son and is assured of God's protection and care. If earthly fathers (who are evil by nature) provide good gifts for their children, how much more will God provide for His children?

God listens to the speech of the righteous and records both their words and works in a "book of remembrance" to be kept before Him. God keeps books of man's deeds, whether they be good or bad. God keeps accurate records of those believers who suffer and undergo trials in staying true to their commitment to the Lord. He even keeps a record of believers' tears shed in times of trouble.

Man's tongue will eventually reveal what is in his heart, "for of the abundance of the heart his mouth speaketh" (Lk. 6:45). In the day of judgment, man will have to give an account

117

of every idle word he speaks. Many believers live as if God is deaf to their conversation and blind to their actions, but He catches and records every word and deed.

The Messianic Hope

His Coming

Malachi revealed the coming of the Messiah in Malachi 3:1. The words "before me . . . saith the LORD of hosts" indicate that God is speaking of the Messiah, for the "me" is connected with "Lord," and "the messenger of the covenant" is the Messiah (God's Son). The second "LORD" is God the Father, who is doing the speaking, showing a plurality in the Godhead. Here we have a clear passage on the Messiah's divinity.

The phrase "shall suddenly [unexpectedly] come to his temple" (v. 1) could be applied to the Messiah's First Coming (Lk. 2:21-38; Mt. 21:12-13; Jn. 2:14-16), but the verse actually refers to Messiah's Second Coming, when His judgment will fall on all unrighteous men. The concept clearly supports this interpretation. Scripture is replete with passages that declare the Second Coming of Christ to bring judgment on the ungodly and establish a righteous kingdom on earth (e.g., Zech. 14:1-9; Rev. 19:11-16; 20:6).

His Cleansing

At the Messiah's coming He will bring cleansing "like a refiner's fire, and like fullers' soap" (3:2). Fire is used to purge the dross from metal. Soap, mixed with water, is used to scrub the dirt from garments. In like manner, after the Messiah's return, He will regather the Jewish people from every land and take them into the wilderness, where He will purge all rebels from the righteous. Only the righteous of Israel will enter the Kingdom; the same will be true when He judges the Gentile nations, separating the sheep from the goats.

Christians will return to the earth with the Lord in their glorified bodies and enjoy the many blessings promised in the

Kingdom age. The Church, along with a redeemed Israel, will rule and reign with Christ for a thousand years.

His Condemnation

In Malachi 3:5, the prophet named four categories of sins that bring swift judgment from God: sorcery (witchcraft), adultery, false swearing (perjury), and defrauding the defenseless in society. Those who practice such sins are cursed. If repentance was not forthcoming, Judah would be set apart for extermination. The same curse will be experienced by the nations when Christ destroys the wicked at His Second Coming.

Today man lives under the curse of sin. He can be delivered from God's judgment only through faith in Jesus the Messiah, who redeemed both Jew and Gentile from the curse of the Law so that the blessing of salvation might be experienced by all who receive Him as Messiah.

The Day of the Lord

In Malachi 4, the prophet mentioned several events that will take place during "the day of the LORD" (v. 5). This day will begin after the Rapture of the Church and cover the time of the Tribulation, concluding with the Great White Throne Judgment.

The Lord is called the "Sun of righteousness" (4:2). When He returns, His brightness will destroy the wicked but bring light and life to the righteous. Light is like a laser: It can be used to destroy or to heal.

In the Kingdom age, the righteousness of both God the Father and Jesus Christ the Son will shine on the believer. Christ, who is called the "day star" (2 Pet. 1:19) and the "bright and morning star" (Rev. 22:16), will shine on the righteous as an everlasting light.

At the end of my preface to this book, I mentioned that Malachi was the final authentic voice of prophecy until John the Baptist shattered the silence 400 years later with the words,

"Repent; for the kingdom of heaven is at hand" (Mt. 3:2). Possibly you have read through this book, but you are unsure of your eternal destiny. Many years may pass before you again hear the words, "Repent; for the kingdom of heaven is at hand." You can make sure you will spend eternity in Heaven by receiving Jesus the Messiah as your Savior. Why not bow before Him in repentance and accept Jesus as your personal Savior and Lord. You can settle it now!

RECOMMENDED READING

Baldwin, Joyce G. *Haggai, Zechariah, Malachi*. The Tyndale Old Testament Commentaries. Downers Grove, IL: Inter-Varsity Press, 1972.

Bullock, C. Hassell. *An Introduction to the Old Testament Prophetic Books*. Chicago: Moody, 1986.

Deane, W. J. "Malachi," *The Pulpit Commentary*, Vol. 14. Grand Rapids, MI: Eerdmans, 1950.

Falwell, Jerry. *Liberty Bible Commentary*. Nashville, TN: Thomas Nelson, 1983.

Feinberg, Charles L. *The Minor Prophets*. Chicago: Moody, 1976.

Freeman, Hobard E. *Introduction to the Old Testament Prophets*. Chicago: Moody, 1968.

Goddard, Burton E. "Malachi," *The Wycliffe Bible Commentary*. Chicago: Moody, 1962.

Hailey, Homer. *A Commentary on the Minor Prophets*. Grand Rapids, MI: Baker, 1972.

Hengstenberg, E. W. "The Prophet Malachi," *Christology of the Old Testament*. Grand Rapids, MI: Kregel, 1970.

Kaiser, Walter C., Jr. *Malachi: God's Unchanging Love*. Grand Rapids, MI: Baker, 1984.

Keil, Carl Friedrich. *The Twelve Minor Prophets*, Vol. 2. Trans. James Martin. Grand Rapids, MI: Eerdmans, 1954.

Laetsch, Theo. *The Minor Prophets*, 2 vols. Repr. Grand Rapids, MI: Baker, 1950.

Morgan, G. Campbell. *Malachi's Message for Today*. Repr. Grand Rapids, MI: Baker, 1972.

Pusey, E.B. *The Minor Prophets*, Vol. 2. Repr. Grand Rapids, MI: Baker, 1950.

Robinson, George L. *The Twelve Minor Prophets*. Repr. Grand Rapids, MI: Baker, 1952.

Tatford, Frederick A. *The Minor Prophets*, Vol. 3. Repr. Minneapolis: Klock & Klock, 1982.

Unger, Merrill F. *Unger's Commentary on the Old Testament*, Vol. 2. Chicago: Moody, 1981.

Willmington, H. L. *Willmington's Guide to the Bible*. Wheaton, IL: Tyndale, 1981.

Wolf, Herbert. *Haggai and Malachi: Rededication and Renewal*. Chicago: Moody, 1976.